Mission: Africa

A FIELD GUIDE

TRANSIT

www.TransitBooks.com

Mission: Africa: A Field Guide
Copyright © 2003 by W Publishing Group

Published by W Publishing Group, a Thomas Nelson Company,
P.O. Box 141000, Nashville, TN 37214

Compiled by Kate Etue and Recah Theodosiou
Cover Design by Matt Lehman at Anderson Thomas Design, Nashville, TN
Page Design by Walter Petrie at Book and Graphic Design, Nashville, TN

Unless otherwise indicated, Scripture quotations used in this book are from the Holy Bible, New Century Version, copyright © 1987, 1988, 1991 by Word Publishing, Dallas, Texas 75234. Used by permission.

Other Scripture references are from the Holy Bible, New International Version (NIV). Copyright © 1973, 1978, 1984, International Bible Society. Used by permission of Zondervan.

The statistics provided in this book may no longer be accurate, as they change daily. Please visit www.unaids.org for the most up-to-date information.

The perspectives, beliefs, and views of individual contributors do not necessarily reflect those of Thomas Nelson, Inc., or W Publishing Group.

Library of Congress Cataloging-in-Publication Data

Mission Africa : a field guide / compiled by Kate Etue and Recah Theodosiou.
    p. cm.
    Summary: A compendium of articles by various authors plus practical suggestions for ways of contributing to the solution of the AIDS crisis in Africa, such as contacting members of Congress and the press and mobilizing local churches.
    ISBN 0-8499-4426-0 (softcover)
    1. AIDS (Disease)—Africa—Juvenile literature. [1. AIDS (Disease) 2. Diseases.]
I. Etue, Kate. II. Theodosiou, Recah.
RA643.86.A35M575 2003
362.1'969792'0096—dc21

                                      2003003709

Printed and bound in the United States of America

03 04 05 06 07 PHX 5 4 3 2

Contents

CONTENTS

Foreword

MICHAEL W. SMITH

S ome of the greatest lessons I have learned in life were from dying children at a hospital in Swetta, South Africa. Most of these children had already lost their parents and soon would lose their own lives. In the midst of their plight—actually in spite of their plight—peace and dignity remained. They each had worth and value in the midst of abject poverty.

The beautiful and rugged continent of Africa has suffered many trials throughout history, and today is no exception. Our brothers and sisters there face disease, poor economies, tribal war, and racism. AIDS is the everyday threat there—killing mothers, husbands, pastors, teachers . . . and children. Five people die every minute in Africa from this disease. In America we have the resources and drugs to help these people live. They don't have to die. They can live long and productive lives with HIV.

Why aren't we doing more? Why isn't news of this pandemic in the media more often? It's been easy for us to turn our eyes away from these people, our neighbors. We haven't been loving them the way Christ commanded us to love others. But what can we really do to help them while we're in Nashville, Omaha, San Diego, New York?

That's why I'm so glad you've picked up *Mission: Africa*. Hopefully this book will encourage, equip, and motivate you to get involved in your own creative way to help fight the AIDS pandemic. So many of your favorite artists and musicians are supporting you in this fight. At the back of the book, you'll find a section called "What Can I Do To Help?" It will give you the step-by-step plans to call your senator, organize a fund-raising campaign, or even take the courageous step of going to Africa as an individual or group.

I believe that you can help to reduce HIV / AIDS in Africa and the world. Make this your mission. Do something bold. It's time to make a difference.

Michael W. Smith
Nasvhille, Tennessee
January 2003

What Will Become of Africa's AIDS Orphans?

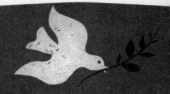

Melissa Fay Greene

F our years ago, a fifth grader in my children's elementary
school in Atlanta lost his father in a twin-engine private
plane crash. The terrible news whipped through the community;
hundreds attended the funeral. Even today, there is a wisp of
tragedy about the tall, blond high school freshman—fatherless,
at so young an age. I find myself thinking about him when sur-
veying the playground of one of the countless hole-in-the-wall
orphanages of Addis Ababa, Ethiopia.

Behind corrugated iron walls off a dirt road, schoolgirls in
donated clothing are throwing pebbles and waggling their long
legs out behind them in hopscotch. Other girls sit on kitchen
chairs in the shade of a cement wall, braiding and rebraiding one
another's hair. They weave plastic beads in arrangements so tight
that the completed hairdo looks like an abacus. Boys lope back
and forth with a half-deflated soccer ball.

Virtually all of these children have lost both parents, most to
AIDS. Malaria, yellow fever, and especially TB are fatal illnesses
here, too. The children's grandparents have also died or are too
poor and sick to care for the children; the same is true of their
aunts and uncles, their neighbors and teachers. But no single one

Do you know anyone personally whose parents are no longer living? How has this affected them and how they relate to others?

of these children has been isolated by tragedy: Being orphaned is one of the common experiences of their generation. Ethiopia has one of the world's largest populations infected with HIV and AIDS. The number of AIDS orphans in Ethiopia is estimated at a million, most of whom end up living on the streets.

But in a hierarchy among orphans, those here at Layla House are the most fortunate. They are HIV negative and healthy, and they have landed in one of two excellent American adoption programs in this city, both generating high interest among prospective adoptive parents in the United States. But they have been plucked out of immeasurable tragedy.

"This is the most devastating pandemic to sweep the earth for many centuries," says Dr. Mark Rosenberg, executive director of the Atlanta-based Task Force for Child Survival and Development. He compares the moral imperative to stop the epidemic in Africa, Asia, and South America to the era of the Holocaust and imagines that future generations will ask, "What did you do to help?"

When I visit one on one with some of the children in a cool cinder-block storeroom, I discover that each is more like the fatherless Atlanta boy than not. As a group, the children generate a carefree mood of ruckus and play, but their secret grief coexists with the brave frolicking. Being orphaned may be typical for their peer group, but it pierces each child in a uniquely tragic way. The boys and girls remember and long for their prior lives, their deceased families, their homes—whether middle-class house or rural hut—and their childhoods that once were normal.

Yemisrach is a big-boned, innocent-faced fifteen- or sixteen-year-old. "I live with my parents until age nine," she says. "We are two girls, two boys. First Mother died; then Father died of malaria. I become like a mother to the others."

Though they try to hold on to their memories, it is possible that the children don't have all of their facts straight. But no one is left to correct them, and the child becomes the family historian.

"My father drink too much, and he fall on the gate, and he get a stone on his head, and he went to the hospital and died," says sweet, worried-looking Yirgalem, whose forehead is too creased for his young age. "After that, he buried."

Robel is a rambunctious eight-year-old of the half-baked-schoolwork type. It is easy to picture him as a bike-riding, Nintendo-loving American boy. He has surmised that hospital treatment killed his mother. "I was born in Tigray," he says, speaking through a translator like most of the younger kids. "Then went with my parents to Sudan as refugees. My father would get food from the refugee camp and bring it to the house. Mother died in Sudan. She went to hospital for injection. First injection is good; second time, she is tired; third injection, she died. Then I hear people crying about Father. They said, 'Your father has died.'

"My small sister, Gelila, is four. When Gelila see something in my hand, she cry, so I give her. She does not remember our parents."

There is a terrible sameness to the stories. They all head down the same path: the mother's death, then the father's; or Father died, then Mother, then small Sister, then funny baby Brother.

Take a moment to pray for the orphaned
children of Africa. Pray for their
health, their comfort, and relief from
their sorrow.

Alone, bringing out the words of the family's end, a child's eyes fill with tears; the chest fills with sobs. Bedtime is the worst, when all shenanigans die down. At night, ghosts and visions and bad dreams visit the children. Through the open windows, you can hear kids crying into their pillows.

The orphans are not confined to the cities. In small farming towns hundreds of miles outside of Addis Ababa, children rush cars, offering flip-flops, bars of soap, packages of tissue, or tree branches heavy with nuts. Those with nothing to sell offer labor: They will wash your windshield or watch your car for you if you park it. Some of these children are, at very young ages, the sole wage earner for their families. Orphaned in the countryside, they have migrated to the villages and towns where they have become squatters, trying to feed themselves and their younger siblings in alley dwellings improvised from scrap lumber or cloth or plastic.

"Almost without exception, children orphaned by AIDS are marginalized, stigmatized, malnourished, uneducated, and psychologically damaged," Carol Bellamy, executive director of UNICEF, said in Namibia. "They are affected by actions over which they have no control and in which they had no part. They deal with the most trauma, face the most dangerous threats, and have the least protections. And because of all this, they, too, are very likely to become HIV positive." She warned that the grow-ing numbers of AIDS orphans means that the world will see "an explosion in the number of child prostitutes, children living on the streets, and child domestic workers."

Eight-year-old Mekdalawit, from Dire Dawa, living in Layla House, remembers the days of her parents' deaths: "My sister Biruktawit is a baby lying on the floor with her feet in the air—like this. Our older sister throw herself in front of the car and scream and yell that she wants to die if our father is dead. Then our mother becomes so ill that she cannot move from her bed. She cannot eat, and she has sores all over her body, and she loves for us to gently scratch her skin."

UNICEF (United Nations Children's Fund) has been helping children around the world for more than fifty-five years. To find out how you can get involved in the work they are doing, log on to www.unicef.org.

Mekdalawit and Biruktawit's eight older siblings tried to raise them, but they were obliged to leave home each day for school and for jobs. Worried that the youngest two would wander away from the family hut and be lost, the older children warned that monsters would catch and eat little girls if they didn't stay inside. Finally, a few of the oldest brought the youngest two to the local authorities who referred them to the Children, Youth, and Family Affairs Department, known as the Children's Commission. It placed them in Layla House. The older sisters tearfully promised to visit, but their village is far from the capital.

Enat House in Addis Ababa, not far from Layla House, is run by a husband and wife, Gezahegn Wolde Yohannes and Atsedeweyen Abraham. The children who live here are all HIV positive, the smallest victims of the continent's collision with HIV/AIDS. Not only have they lost their mothers and fathers and siblings, but they themselves are sick. Some of them have begun to lose their hair; others are frighteningly thin; others have facial sores; and all but the babies and toddlers know precisely, in grim detail, what that means.

At Enat, the first clue that the health of another child has taken a downward turn is the child's refusal to enter into the games and exercises she enjoyed last week. A child sitting listlessly on the curb at this playground is an awful omen. The day I visit Enat (an Amharic word for "mother"), the directors and the teachers are mourning the death of a six-year-old boy a few days earlier.

But on the dirt playground, shaded by eucalyptus trees, the little girls weave one another's hair, and the children are awaiting a visit from their beloved guitar-playing PE teacher. The homey sour smell of *injera*—the national bread, a spongy sourdough flat pancake—rises from an outdoor brick kitchen.

Later, in a sunny, freshly mopped dining hall, the children seat themselves at long tables for an art class. A glass vase of cut flowers sparkles with clean water on a tabletop. The children from rural areas have never seen scissors before, and their fingers wiggle with eagerness when the teacher begins handing out brightly colored plastic scissors. Yes, there are enough—Christ Lutheran Church of Forest Hills, Pennsylvania, sent plenty in their boxes of donations. Following instructions, the children generate a blizzard of paper scraps in their first attempts to form snowflakes. (They have never seen snowflakes either.) Stocky little Bettye is a pint-size Ethel Merman with a husky belly laugh and a booming voice. She pokes her tongue out the corner of her mouth as she scissors, in classic kindergarten style. The children hold up their lopsided constructions for one another to see, and they hoot in surprise.

The teacher, a slim woman in a long brown dress and head scarf, murmurs words of praise and often bends to stroke a child on the cheek, a gesture of calming affection. Later I watch a music class, which consists of much hands-on-hip swaying and jumping under the guidance of the guitar-playing young PE teacher. Bettye belts out the words of the songs and jerks her fat little tush around. Eyob is a handsome, endearing boy in baggy brown pants and loafers, who slightly stalls his hand claps and foot stomps till the last moment of each beat; I think he is inventing swing. But Eyob's hair is coming out in tufts. So is Bettye's. And there are no older children at this house; there are no older HIV-positive children at all.

"Our little ones think they are going to America like the children in adoption programs," Atsede says. She is a small, dignified woman with delicate features and fine hair, who stands ramrod straight and offers a mild smile that trembles between civility and grief; she has seen much death. "The older ones gradually understand: 'Because we have AIDS, we cannot go to America.'" In fact, though it is not explicitly U.S. policy to exclude HIV-positive adopted children, and these children generally respond rapidly to the onset of medical treatment in America, the immigration paperwork is more complicated, and few families step forward for these youngsters.

So the Enat children are not in line for adoption; nor are they receiving medical treatment. "Medication to fight AIDS is not available," says Atsede's husband, Gezahegn, who has the dark, rumpled, bloodshot look of a man who has been up all night; he has wrestled AIDS for a dozen of these small lives already and has had every one of them pulled from his arms.

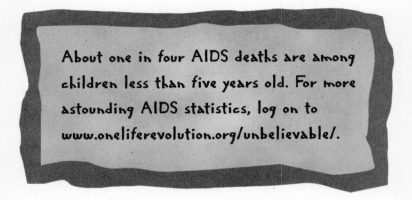

About one in four AIDS deaths are among children less than five years old. For more astounding AIDS statistics, log on to www.oneliferevolution.org/unbelievable/.

In America last year, thanks to vigorous treatment of infected pregnant women, only 200 HIV/AIDS-infected children were born, down from 2,000 in 1994. Most of those babies will live fairly normal lives and survive to adulthood. In Africa, without medications to treat complicating infections, 75 percent of HIV-positive babies will be dead by the age of 2, says Dr. Mark Kline, director of the International Pediatric AIDS Initiative at the Baylor College of Medicine in Houston. Of the remaining 25 percent, he says, very few will reach age 11.

Until recently, Enat served as a holding center for children prior to testing. It was not always clear at first whether the children were infected or not. "We see nice kids, bright futures, then we must test them," Atsede says. "Some get the news that they are negative; then we can refer them to the Children's Commission for assignment to a foreign adoption program. Some will be adopted to America; others, to different countries. But other children test positive. When they first come, we often cannot guess. You'd think it would be the baby of a sibling group who will test positive, but then the results come back and sometimes it is the middle child, so the older child and the baby are transferred out."

Gezahegn's background was in business and government administration, not medicine; he was reluctant to enter this field. Now he finds it has swallowed his life. Nothing compares in importance with trying to sustain the lives of the ill children in his care. "We can fight pneumonia and small infections in the children, but that is all," he says. "We are running a hospice program. It is rather hard to see the children dying."

Still, these stricken children must be counted among the relatively blessed of their generation; the care they receive is the best available. "The children are happy here," Atsede says. "We celebrate holidays; we give them birthdays; we invite their living relatives to visit them. They know that the children at orphanages with adoption programs are learning English and other languages, so we teach them English here, too, so they don't feel left out. The hotels invite them to swing and climb on their playgrounds. We want them to enjoy life. We want them to see something of life."

Think about your own talents and gifts. Will you be a doctor someday? A teacher? An aid worker? Are there skills you can offer even now to the AIDS cause in Africa?

Time for that is often short. "A child begins by losing weight," Gezahegn says. "Then she develops infections, stops eating, has diarrhea, pain in joints, pain in ears. It can take five months, three months, two months. A child does not talk about it, but she's kind of depressed. One day she is not playing on the playground; she just wants to sit and to be held."

It has become the life mission of this couple to do more than sit by the deathbeds of small children in pain. They are not participants in the debate among health-care professionals over whether treatment or prevention ought to be the public health priority in Africa, Asia, and South America. Their question is simpler: How can they get hold of the triple cocktails that in America now have reduced deaths by AIDS by 76 percent since 1996?

By American standards, the cost doesn't sound extravagant. An average figure for pediatric triple-drug therapy in Africa is now $60 to $80 per child per month, and the price is dropping.

How did you spend your allowance last month? Did you go to the movies? Have pizza with friends? Go on a shopping spree at the mall? For only $60 to $80 per month, a child with AIDS can receive the drug therapy that could save his or her life.

But without serious commitment of financing from the industrialized world, even these modest costs are unreachable.

When Atsede sits down on a chair in the dirt yard under a shade tree for a rare break, the children skitter over to her and lay their heads upon her long cotton skirts or climb up into her arms and nuzzle their faces into her neck. She laughs as her face is dotted with kisses. "The children call me Abaye, Daddy, and her Emaye, Mommy," Gezahegn says. A little girl waits for him, eager to demonstrate for him a trick she has mastered at jump-rope. The music class waits for his attention to show that they have learned a song with synchronized dance steps. Children raise their hands and hop up and down to be chosen by Gezahegn to accompany him in the backfiring van on an errand to town. Until sickness comes, the faces under the bouncing braids of the little girls and the brimmed caps of the boys are round, happy, and hopeful.

"Without therapy," Kline says, "as far as we know, all of the children will die."

Layla House, a shady compound with a paved common area, a baby house, dormitories for boys and for girls, a schoolroom, and a kitchen and dining hall, is run by Adoption Advocates International, based in Port Angeles, Washington. A.F.A.A. House, on the outskirts of town, almost buried in flower gardens, is run by Americans for African Adoptions, based in Indianapolis and directed by Cheryl Carter-Shotts. These two are the only American agencies permitted by the Ethiopian government to arrange for adoption of healthy Ethiopian orphans to America. More than one hundred children joined new families in the U.S. in 2001. At least a dozen other adoption agencies based in Addis Ababa represent Australia, Canada, and seven nations of Western Europe and Scandinavia.

It is the first recourse of everyone ethically involved with intercountry adoption to place orphans with relatives, with friends, or with families within their home countries; no one imagines or pretends that adoption is a solution to a generation of children orphaned by disease. It is one very small and modest option, a case of families in industrialized nations throwing lifelines to individual children even as their governments fail to commit the money to turn back the epidemic. "Consider the impact of *The Diary of Anne Frank* on the world," says Mark Rosenberg. "That was the journal of just one doomed child. Though we are looking at the deaths of millions, the saving of even one life is not trivial."

In the dusty schoolroom at Layla House, students face forward on wood benches and chant lessons in high voices. It is a relief on this hot day to enter the cool, whitewashed room. The children's faces are soft and hopeful. Most are of elementary school age, though a few perspiring teenagers tower over the rest with the same earnest, slightly anxious expressions. Their teacher, a young man who has never been to America—though it is his fondest wish to go—writes American greetings on the chalkboard.

"How are you?" he taps out, while pronouncing the words.

"How are you?" the children repeat.

"I am fine," he dabs in chalk.

"I am fine," they call back in high voices.

"I am very well," he writes.

"I am very well," they sing. They roll their Rs, giving a high-tone flourish to their "verys."

"I am doing nicely."

"I am doing nicely."

There is no preparation for bad news here, I notice. The working premise is that these children will be chosen by American families for adoption, and their airfare out of Ethiopia paid for by their waiting parents. From the vantage point of this ancient and poor country, this great opportunity would seem to leave no room for complaint and thus no need to prepare a vocabulary of grumbling.

"How are you this evening?"

"How are you this evening?"

"I am quite well, thank you."

"I am quite well, thank you."

With the next lesson, the teacher offers many ways to express "I don't know." "I have no idea," the young man is calling over his shoulder. "I have no I-dea," sing the sweet voices, rising up near the end of each phrase. "I shouldn't think so." "I shouldn't think so." "I don't expect so." "I don't expect so." "Search me." "Search me." "I haven't a clue." "I haven't a clue." Through the square, uncovered windows, sunlight and dust motes stream onto the pebbly floor. The kids, wearing T-shirts, cutoffs, and flip-flops, begin to fidget in expectation of lunchtime.

> Write down five things that you and your friends, youth group, or civic organization can do to help the AIDS crisis in Africa. Make a plan to accomplish your goals.

The lessons in Americana do not cease at mealtime. At long wood tables, there are bowls of orange slices and carved-up bread. Though the children would welcome at every meal platters of injera used in lieu of silverware, they are being taught to use American forks and spoons and to maneuver foods like spaghetti and meatballs. "Please to pass the water," a boy booms. "Thank you very much." "Thank you very much," replies his friend, who has passed the pitcher. "How are you this evening?" "I am very well," shouts the roly-poly boy. "How are you this morning?" "I have no idea. Please how is your sister?" "I haven't a clue. Please to pass the meatball. Thank you very much." "Thank you very much."

Some of these kids once lived on the street, cried for food, tried to keep alive younger siblings, and had few prospects of surviving to adulthood without their birth parents. They now enjoy fantasies that they will wear Walkmans and ride bicycles when they live in America. When asked by the adults in their lives, "What do you want to be when you grow up?" no one replies, "I didn't actually realize I was going to grow up," though some must think it. Instead, these boys and girls have learned to reply "doctor," "teacher," "scientist." "I want to drive a car," says a six-year-old girl named Bethlehem; whether professionally or at her leisure, she doesn't specify. "I will be an actor!" cries a boy, "an actor like Jackie Chan." "I want to ride motorcycles!" shouts another boy. "When I grow up, I want to help the elderly people," says a merry dimpled thirteen-year-old girl, Mekdes, cognizant, like many of the young teens, that she is on the receiving end of charity and eager, herself, to be of service.

"I wasn't at all sure what the response of American families would be to our opening an Ethiopian adoption program," says Merrily Ripley, director of Adoption Advocates International. Her agency places children from Haiti, China, and Thailand with American adoptive families and assists with a program focusing on children orphaned in Sierra Leone. She flies to Ethiopia nearly every other month and occasionally indulges the little girls who beg to fix her long, straight gray hair. On this day, she looks like a cross between someone's hippie grandmother and Bo Derek in "10," with skinny beaded braids dangling over her shoulders. "Would we be able to find families for African children? Would we be able to manage a children's home half a world away? We never dreamed that Ethiopia would become our most popular program."

While a couple of the older children have arrived with psychological challenges based on early loss of mother or other relative, the majority began their lives in families as breast-fed, tickled, treasured children. They are like kids in any backyard or school playground in America. Though a round-roofed straw hut in Gondar, Ethiopia may seem impossibly different from a suburban home outside Cleveland or San Francisco, it is not. Children who have known the love of parents are eager to enjoy it again, and their adjustment to American family life has been rapid.

No one grieves openly at Layla House except frightened newcomers. One day, it was four-year-old Isak, an only child whose father died a year earlier and whose mother died just three months before. A kind neighbor walked Isak to the local authorities, who notified the Children's Commission, which placed him here. His head freshly shaved, Isak sat alone on a low curb at the far edge of the playground, mute with homesickness and embarrassment and misery. His round dark eyes looked too big for his bald head; his head looked too big for his body. Although he knew his mother was dead, he couldn't help looking up briefly at every adult, just in case, but the particle of hope in his eyes was nearly extinguished.

On his first night in the boys' dorm room, he shied back from the four sets of white metal bunk beds, but big boys were kind to him; Haptamu and Frew showed Isak that they slept within arm's reach. When he yelped in the night, one of the two sleepily murmured a word of comfort.

Within two weeks, Isak found his niche in the community of children. He made a long detour around the rough playground football game and shyly volunteered, instead, to partake in the traditional Ethiopian coffee ceremony arranged by little girls under the vines, with a wood plank for a table and used bottle caps as cups. His soft curly hair began to grow out; his haunted look softened; and his photograph was privately circulated by

Adoption Advocates International to prospective adoptive families who had signed up with the agency.

Every child on the premises can recite which children have adoptive families waiting for them in America and which children are still hoping to be matched with a family. The assigned children have in their possession small photograph albums full of nearly unbelievable images: big grinning adults—white or African-American—standing on green lawns in front of pretty houses and happy children playing on swing sets, sitting astride ponies, wearing goggles and leaping off diving boards, or appearing in hooded parkas and mittens, pulling sleds up snowy hills. The orphans turn the plastic-covered pages of their photo albums slowly, trying to make sense of each image. These have to be fairy tales! Yet the owner of each album has been told it is his or her destiny to leap into these scenes.

> Consider what you have been given in life. Thank God for all his many blessings. Now pray for his blessing and protection over the orphaned children at Layla House.

"I think America has all things in her hands," says the boy who wants to be Jackie Chan. "Everyone is hoping to be chosen by American parents. When the children learn that they have parents, they tell from peoples to peoples their parents' names and their city."

Though still small, the number of Ethiopian children adopted by Americans has grown substantially in the last ten years.

"What families consistently tell us is how happy and well adjusted the children are, that they obviously had been well nurtured and that they are extremely intelligent," says Carter-Shotts of Americans for African Adoptions.

Some of the children from the countryside arrive in the United States with tribal markings or accidental scars from a cook fire or a goat's horn. Asrat, who is now twenty and was one of the early Ethiopian children to be adopted in this country, killed a lion when he was very young, using a stick from the fire in defense of his family compound. He proudly wore a ritual scar across one eyebrow, bestowed by his village of Welayta, which declared him a man. Within months after his referral to an adoption program, he was a fifth grader at a Seattle-area elementary school.

Samuel, a seven-year-old whose parents died of malaria, missed sleeping on his shelflike bed high under the roof of the family's round hut and listening to the rain scatter when it hit the corrugated metal. Shortly after he was adopted, he graciously asked his suburban mom if she would like him to butcher a cow for dinner.

Abebaw, seven, missed the *doro wat*—the chicken stew—of his homeland after he was adopted by an American family in South Korea. His mother, Anna, brought home chunks of cut-up chicken from the grocery.

"No, real chicken, you need," he protested.

"This is real chicken," she said.

"No, need real chicken. Ethiopia chicken."

"OK, I give up. What is real chicken?"

"The kind you cut head off. Noisy one. Running around. Head off, but running. That Ethiopia chicken."

Yilkal, ten, was adopted by an African-American family in Katy, Texas. One quarter of Adoption Advocates International's adoptive families for Ethiopian kids are African-American or Ethiopian-American. When Yilkal's mother, Naomi Talley, flew to Addis Ababa to meet him and take him home, her hosts all praised her beauty and said that her forebears must have come from Ethiopia. Once settled with his new father, mother, and younger sister into an upscale American house on a cul-de-sac, Yilkal revised his personal saga and told his new friends and teachers that the entire Talley family had just emigrated from Ethiopia. Naomi was startled when a local organization of African émigrés left a welcome basket on the doorstep and an invitation to a picnic. "They'll know," she told her son, laughing. "I don't speak Amharic or any other African language."

"They won't know, Mama," he pleaded, looking at her adoringly.

Biruktawit and Mekdalawit, the little sisters with the eight older siblings, were referred by the Children's Commission to Adoption Advocates International and were adopted by Bob and Chris Little in Port Townsend, Washington. Chris, a petite blonde with a Peter Pan haircut, recently lingered at the doorway of the girls' bedroom and overheard Mekdalawit, now called Marta, loudly praying: "Thank you, God, for my mom. She's a good, good mom. She knows how to be a good mom. Even when I mad, she love me. Even when I sad, she love me. Even when I do bad thing, she love me. My mom, she so cute. My mom, she not ugly. But she ugly, I still love her. Even if she ugly, I love her. Even if she really ugly, I love her. And she love me, if she ugly. But she not; she cute. Thank you, thank you, God, for good and cute mom."

Meanwhile, the Children's Commission is referring orphans to both American-run orphanages in Addis, as well as to the city's other orphanages, foster homes, and adoption programs. The referrals come to numbers far greater than can be housed by the existing institutions. Adoptive families are desperately sought, for each international program is like a finger in the dike, beyond which brims an inconceivably rising flood of orphaned, homeless, healthy children.

Last year, Helen, a shy and tiny five-year-old with huge eyes and a high-pitched squeak of a voice, was handed a package on the orphanage playground telling her that she had been matched with an adoptive family in America. It was my husband and I who had prepared the presents while waiting for approval from the Ethiopian courts to bring Helen to America as our daughter. We have loved raising our children—four by birth and one by adoption; when we began to muse about adopting again, it seemed logical to think about Africa, described in newspapers as "a continent of orphans."

"Be careful. Don't think these little children are worth nothing. I tell you that they have angels in heaven who are always with my Father in heaven."
Matthew 18:10

Hair ribbons, two pastel-colored plastic ponies with brushable hair, a photograph album, turquoise sunglasses, and a pink T-shirt that said "Atlanta" spilled out of Helen's envelope that day, five months before I visited. An adoptive mother at the orphanage to take home her child delivered Helen's package and took pictures of the moment. So many kids shoved and grabbed to see Helen's photo album that it flew out of her grasp and traveled the length and breadth of the playground. Big boys called out approving comments to her. Though she couldn't get her book back, no one damaged it, and she contented herself with the ponies, allowing her best friend to brush one of them. Finally one of the big boys said, "Here, Helen," and gave the book back, and Helen tucked herself away on her lower bunk bed and examined the faces of white people who had labeled the pictures: "Your Big Sister," "Your Oldest Sister," "Your Brothers," "Our Dog," "Your Bedroom," "Your Father," "Your Mother." She looked at them with, and without, the turquoise sunglasses.

Helen's parents had lovingly reared their only child, taught her to read Amharic and English at age four, planned for her future, and were separated from her by only illness and death. I learned of their devotion to her from friends of the family, who looked after Helen but were too old to adopt her. Before going to sleep on the night she received her package from America, Helen propped open her photo album on the bedside table to the page showing the new "Mommy and Daddy" arm in arm, laughing and dressed in fine clothes. She laid her head carefully on the pillow facing the picture and fell asleep looking at it. It became her bedtime ritual.

A few months later, I came to Ethiopia to meet Helen. She had been told I was planning to adopt her, though the completion of the process was still many months away. When I showed up at the orphanage for the first time, she was too shy and alarmed to look at me. I pulled bags of rocket balloons out of my purse— they blow up into long blimps, and when you release them, they zoom around and make embarrassing noises. The children began running wildly after them and screaming with laughter. I saw Helen watching us from across the playground, and for the first time in my presence, she laughed.

Although her hair was tightly, beautifully beaded and braided, she wore well-used boys' orphanage clothes. A driver I had hired, Selamneh, and I took her shopping at a children's store one evening, a boutique so small that most of its wares— toys and clothing—hung from hooks high up on the ceiling. Helen instantly took possession of the shop. She shrieked with happiness and quickly pointed out her desires: a pair of shiny red sandals, an electric guitar, a toy gun, a bicycle, and a wedding dress. I said yes to the sandals, no to the rest, and pulled a different dress off the rack to show her. She turned her little nose up at it just like my children at home, who never appreciate my taste, and she selected her own dress, a complicated affair involving several layers and embroidered sheep.

> Remember your last birthday? What sorts of gifts did you receive? Were you gracious and thankful to those who gave you presents? Consider what just one of those gifts might have meant to a child in Africa.

She also bought pajamas, underwear, play clothes, and lacy socks with attached pink flowers. She opted to wear the socks to the apartment we stayed in during my visit. That night she scrubbed her new socks in the bathroom sink for half an hour, then hung them outside on the balcony to dry.

I opened a box of raisins one afternoon and handed her one. She examined it and ate it, and I ate one, too. Then I gave her the box of raisins to keep, and she zipped it into her new American backpack. A few nights later, she and I were dinner guests at the home of an Ethiopian family. Helen excused herself from dinner at one point, went to find her backpack, unzipped it, extracted the box of raisins, carefully opened it, and with great seriousness handed each person in the family one raisin before replacing the box. That's how they do it in America, she figured.

Last February, Merrily Ripley escorted Helen to the Atlanta airport, where my husband and I went to greet her and to take her home. She had memorized the photo album we had sent her and knew the names of the three older brothers, the two older sisters, and the dog. She was too shy to speak to anyone other than nine-year-old Lily, who was closest to her in age, to whom she whispered in Amharic. (Alas, Lily could not understand a word of it.) An Ethiopian friend in Atlanta visited every day to chat with Helen. "I feel happy," Helen told her in Amharic during that first week. And, "I forget the name of the tall brother." And, "I don't like cheese."

Seth, seventeen, was enormously tall to Helen, but on her third night in America, she snatched a sock off his foot and fled shrieking with it through the house. He gave chase. She ran past me at one point, her face flushed with excitement, threw me the sock to hide, and then ran up the stairs to escape. When Seth finally ambushed her and pried open her hands and searched her pockets, he discovered she didn't have the sock anymore, and she cackled with laughter. The next morning, she tried his name aloud. "Tzetz!" she yelled, then dove under the kitchen table with stage fright.

She quickly adopted the American attitude that there is no problem technology cannot solve, including the fact that she didn't know how to swim. On repeated trips to the drugstore, she gathered essential items for weeks before the neighborhood pool opened, and on opening day, she emerged from the locker room encased in a foam life jacket, arm floaties, scuba-diving goggles, snorkle, and pink flippers. She flip-flopped to pool's edge and bravely dropped into the water. She wore so much equipment that she bobbed along the surface like a water bug, unable to submerge herself. Finally she pitched forward and dunked her head, so all that was visible was a tiny rear end moving across the pool like that of an upended duckling searching for fish underwater.

Another time, Helen showed up at my bedside in the middle of the night, saying, "I had a bad dream."

I opened the covers. "Come, lie here. Go back to sleep, and you'll have a good dream."

"How do you have a good dream?" she asked.

"Well, you think of a happy place, and then you'll dream about the happy place. When I was small, I used to imagine a little place in the forest where animals lived."

"Oh, OK!" she yelled. "I've got one! Guess!"

I so wanted to go back to sleep, but there seemed no way around it. "Is it the beach?"

"No!"

"The forest, with the little animals?"

"No!"

"Somewhere in Ethiopia?"

"No! Can it be a store?"

"Helen!" I said, already knowing.

"It's Target!" she cried and snuggled down for a good sleep.

But it hasn't all been happiness. For at least an hour a day, for the first month after arrival, Helen was consumed by grief. We could see it coming on from a distance; we could see her trying to resist the approaching waves of sorrow. Finally they would overwhelm her, and she would begin to suck and suck and suck in air. Huge sobs and tears shook her, but she allowed us to try to comfort her. We would hold her, and she would wail with sadness.

Our Ethiopian friend translated for us that she was homesick for her friends at Layla House. Adoption Advocates International sponsors an annual reunion of Ethiopian kids adopted by American families. This summer, Helen was reunited with many of her pals from Addis, and I easily promised her that many more are coming to America and she will see them again.

But eight-year-old Eyob, the tap-dancing boy, was also her friend. They lived in the same orphanage for a while after losing their mothers, before blood tests separated them. "This is my friend," she says about Eyob's photo, laughing to remember how funny he is. But Eyob is HIV positive and living at Enat, and Enat has no drugs. I can't promise my daughter that she will see Eyob again since he, like so many others, has been left to die.

> "We must not become tired of doing good. We will receive our harvest of eternal life at the right time if we do not give up." Galatians 6:9

One day not long ago, she collapsed in my arms to cry about her late mother. I held her as she writhed, wailing, "Why she had to die?" A few moments later, she said, amid tears: "I know why she died. Because she was very sick, and we didn't have the medicine."

"I know," I said. "It's true. I'm so sorry. I wish I had known you then. I wish I could have sent her the medicine."

"But we didn't have a phone," she cried, "and I couldn't call you."

Helen has made lots of friends in America and loves to chat, in fluent English, with all her new neighbors and classmates. I always hear her ask, near the start of every play date, "Do you have a mother?" If she is feeling shy, she will whisper to me, "Does she have a mother?" Most children and adults are surprised by the question—"Of course I have a mother!" they reply—but African friends are not surprised. Helen has a mother again now, too, as she is eager to tell, but she doesn't take it as a given about anyone.

The First to Help

OUT OF EDEN

O ur desire to be involved in the AIDS crisis stems from our African roots. Our families are from South Africa, so we have always had a heart for its people. We have experienced first-hand the devastation that has been going on there. Something must be done. We must be proactive.

Recently, we partnered with World Vision, an organization with a heart for the AIDS crisis, to sponsor 100 African kids at our concerts. At $26 per month per child, we have had a great response. We have also teamed up with the DATA organization. We have encouraged people to get involved by signing petitions at our concerts—petitions that go to Congress to ask that they vote

For more information on how you can sponsor a child through World Vision, log on to www.worldvision.org.

to drop Africa's debt and add money to the budget to support the AIDS crisis. We want people to continue adding their names to these petitions. We want them to write to their congressmen. We aren't always able to take money out of our pockets, but our government can.

The biggest responsibility, however, lies not with the government but with the believers of the world. I appeal to all Christians who read this to live as Jesus lived, walk as Jesus walked. The Bible tells us that Jesus instructed his disciples to love their neighbors and give to the poor. He urged believers who professed his name to help those less fortunate than themselves. Yet, over time, Christians have put these things aside. We have forgotten what the Bible says. We have not done our job in loving our neighbors. We, as believers, need to abandon our hypocrisy and set the example. We must be the first to help those in need.

Written for The aWAKE Project, *copyright © 2002 by Andrea Baca.*

Interview with Teron Carter

GRITS

 Good morning, Teron.
Good morning!

Thanks for talking with us about the AIDS crisis in Africa. What made you decide to support awareness for this crisis?

We have come to a point in our own lives where we feel we must look for opportunities to be a part of solutions, change, and empowerment when it comes to social, national, and worldwide issues such as in this case.

You're in a place of influence in our culture. Why do you think America's youth should care about the crisis?

As future leaders of the world, we have to nourish our sense of global concerns within the process of our educational and economical priorities. If I'm not mistaken, the very reason we are even in the company of the wealthiest countries is because of our international trading and assistance to other nations.

What can your fans do on a day-to-day basis to make a difference?

There are several things that can be done, like contacting specific government officials (city, state, and national), finding local organizations to partner with to raise awareness, and making a conscious effort to continue to be informed.

Have you written to your congressperson or other government officials to voice your opinion on the AIDS crisis in Africa? If not, do it now.

Why are you passionate about this issue as opposed to abortion, homelessness, or any other issue?

The same passion is there for many issues—this one is just in a state of emergency and at such a magnitude it's hard not to pay closer attention.

So we've got to act quickly. Isn't it right that five people die every minute? That's like fifteen people just during the time it's taking people to read this article.

You're right. People need to act now and with passion. An entire generation could die right in front of us if we don't decide to help.

What is the most important thing teens need to know about this crisis?

In my opinion, it's that we have solutions, but it's going to take everyone's effort and involvement in order to see them go into effect, no matter what your status is.

Finally, why should Christians specifically care about this issue and these people?

The very foundation of the faith is built on the principle of selflessness. It should be a natural burden in the heart of a true disciple of Christ or believer to do something for the millions who are dying.

Interview for Mission: Africa, *copyright © 2003 by Teron Carter.*

Twenty-First-Century Miracle Man

KEVIN MAX, DC TALK

The face of Christ is not the face of prosperity. It is not the face of comfort or of the church. The sharp lines and haunted eyes are of sorrow, the brow of hope, and the chin of confidence. The face of Christ knows poverty and is familiar with rejection, ignorance, and hatred. When I think of a picture of a modern Jesus, a twenty-first-century miracle man, my internal eye sees these things. My inner-mind portrait would be of a man undernourished yet strong. He would be full of compassion, magic, and mystery, a rebel with a cause. This portrait would involve the controversial settings of his social agenda. Instead of well-dressed, comfortable, fattened faces, he would be surrounded by lepers, prostitutes, and men of low stature. The destitute knew him and called him *friend*. The common sinner felt the brush of his hand and the power of his love. The leper, thief, and demon-possessed knew his name, not by circumstance but by relationship.

The face of Christ is the face of utter, shameless love and grace. It is a temple of acceptance, a warm skull of familiarity. When I think of a twenty-first-century Jesus, I see a friend to the AIDS victim, a person of humility and understanding. If I had to search for him, I would start in the streets and alleyways of the restless.

I would find him in the mists of Africa.

I would find him seeking me.

When I think of all the ignorance and hatred in the world, all of the injustice, I think of the Nazarene strung up on a cross. "No man can come to the Father, but through *me*," he said time and time again. I have to believe this same Jesus opens his arms time and time again to the orphans and victims of AIDS. I am like you; I live in a comfortable home, drive a nice car, and watch movies from a DVD player. In fact, I found out about the AIDS in Africa crisis not through the church but from the lips of a rock-'n'-roll star. I am guilty of living well, and in comfort, and hiding within the shadows of our majestic American steeples. I would hope we could walk out of our comfort, once in a while, to feel the heat of truth on our faces.

With the falling of the two towers and the rising of hatred in the Middle East, there are many opportunities for prayer. I have felt the need to see the plight of Africa with my own eyes, but for a time will do what I can through prayer and intercession.

This is something we all can do, something we were made to do. We can affect culture and we can make a difference: Flesh and blood were made for soul work.

The face of Christ is not the face of prosperity; it is the face of giving.

Written for The aWAKE Project, *copyright © 2002 by Kevin Max.*

Death Stalks a Continent

Johanna McGeary

In the dry timber of African societies, AIDS was a spark. The conflagration it set off continues to kill millions. Here's why.

Imagine your life this way.

You get up in the morning and breakfast with your three kids. One is already doomed to die in infancy. Your husband works two hundred miles away, comes home twice a year, and sleeps around in between. You risk your life in every act of sexual intercourse. You go to work past a house where a teenager lives alone, tending young siblings without any source of income. At another house, the wife was branded a whore when she asked her husband to use a condom, beaten silly, and thrown into the streets. Over there lies a man desperately sick without access to a doctor or clinic or medicine or food or blankets or even a kind word. At work you eat with colleagues, and every third one is already fatally ill. You whisper about a friend who admitted she had the plague and whose neighbors stoned her to death. Your leisure is occupied by the funerals you attend every Saturday. You go to bed fearing adults your age will not live into their forties. You and your neighbors and your political and popular leaders act as if nothing is happening.

33

Start a "Pray for Africa" e-mail prayer chain. Send weekly updates about the growing needs there and offer practical ways for all on your list to become personally involved.

Across the southern quadrant of Africa, this nightmare is real. The word not spoken is *AIDS,* and here at ground zero of humanity's deadliest cataclysm, the ultimate tragedy is that so many people don't know—or don't want to know—what is happening.

As the HIV virus sweeps mercilessly through these lands—the fiercest trial Africa has yet endured—a few try to address the terrible depredation. The rest of society looks away. Flesh and muscle melt from the bones of the sick in packed hospital wards and lonely bush kraals. Corpses stack up in morgues until those on top crush the identity from the faces underneath. Raw earth mounds scar the landscape, grave after grave without name or number. Bereft children grieve for parents lost in their prime, for siblings scattered to the winds.

The victims don't cry out. Doctors and obituaries do not give the killer its name. Families recoil in shame. Leaders shirk responsibility. The stubborn silence heralds victory for the disease: Denial cannot keep the virus at bay.

The developed world is largely silent, too. AIDS in Africa has never commanded the full-bore response the West has brought to other, sometimes lesser, travails. We pay sporadic attention, turning on the spotlight when an international conference occurs, then turning it off. Good-hearted donors donate; governments acknowledge that more needs to be done. But think how different the effort would be if what is happening here were happening in the West.

By now you've seen pictures of the sick, the dead, the orphans. You've heard appalling numbers: the number of new infections, the number of the dead, the number who are sick without care, the number walking around already fated to die.

But to comprehend the full horror AIDS has visited on Africa, listen to the woman we have dubbed Laetitia Hambahlane in Durban or the boy Tsepho Phale in Francistown or the woman who calls herself Thandiwe in Bulawayo or Louis Chikoka, a long distance trucker. You begin to understand how AIDS has struck Africa—with a biblical virulence that will claim tens of millions of lives—when you hear about shame and stigma and ignorance and poverty and sexual violence and migrant labor and promiscuity and political paralysis and the terrible silence that surrounds all this dying. It is a measure of the silence that some asked us not to print their real names to protect their privacy.

Theirs is a story about what happens when a disease leaps the confines of medicine to invade the body politic, infecting not just individuals but an entire society. As AIDS migrated to man in Africa, it mutated into a complex plague with confounding social, economic, and political mechanics that locked together to accelerate the virus's progress. The region's social dynamics colluded to spread the disease and help block effective intervention.

We have come to three countries abutting one another at the bottom of Africa—Botswana, South Africa, Zimbabwe—the heart of the heart of the epidemic. For nearly a decade, these nations suffered a hidden invasion of infection that concealed the dimension of the coming calamity. Now the omnipresent dying reveals the shocking scale of the devastation.

AIDS in Africa bears little resemblance to the American epidemic, limited to specific high-risk groups and brought under control through intensive education, vigorous political action, and expensive drug therapy. Here the disease has bred a Darwinian perversion. Society's fittest, not its frailest, are the ones who die—adults spirited away, leaving the old and the children behind. You cannot define risk groups: Everyone who is sexually active is at risk. Babies too, unwittingly infected by mothers. Barely a single family remains untouched. Most do not know how or when they caught the virus, many never know they have it, many who do know don't tell anyone as they lie dying. Africa can provide no treatment for those with AIDS.

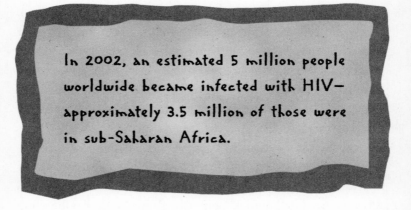

In 2002, an estimated 5 million people worldwide became infected with HIV—approximately 3.5 million of those were in sub-Saharan Africa.

They will all die of tuberculosis, pneumonia, meningitis, diarrhea, whatever overcomes their ruined immune systems first. And the statistics, grim as they are, may be too low. There is no broad-scale AIDS testing: Infection rates are calculated mainly from the presence of HIV in pregnant women. Death certificates in these countries do not record AIDS as the cause. "Whatever stats we have are not reliable," warns Mary Crewe of the University of Pretoria's Center for the Study of AIDS. "Everybody's guessing."

THE OUTCAST

To acknowledge AIDS in yourself is to be branded as monstrous. Laetitia Hambahlane (not her real name) is fifty-one and sick with AIDS. So is her brother. She admits it; he doesn't. In her mother's broken-down house in the mean streets of Umlazi township, Laetitia's mother hovers over her son, nursing him, protecting him, resolutely denying he has anything but TB, though his sister claims the sure symptoms of AIDS mark him. Laetitia is the outcast, first from her family, then from her society.

For years Laetitia worked as a domestic servant in Durban and dutifully sent all her wages home to her mother. She fell in love a number of times and bore four children. "I loved that last man," she recalls. "After he left, I had no one, no sex." That was 1992, but Laetitia already had HIV.

She fell sick in 1996, and her employers sent her to a private doctor who couldn't diagnose an illness. He tested her blood and found she was HIV positive. "I wish I'd died right then," she says, as tears spill down her sunken cheeks. "I asked the doctor, 'Have you got medicine?' He said no. I said, 'Can't you keep me alive?'" The doctor could do nothing and sent her away. "I couldn't face the world," she says. "I couldn't sleep at night. I sat on my bed, thinking, praying. I did not see anyone day or night. I ask God, Why?"

Laetitia's employers fired her without asking her exact diagnosis. For weeks she could not muster the courage to tell anyone. Then she told her children, and they were ashamed and frightened. Then, harder still, she told her mother. Her mother raged about the loss of money if Laetitia could not work again. She was so angry she ordered Laetitia out of the house. When her daughter wouldn't leave, the mother threatened to sell the house to get rid of her daughter. Then she walled off her daughter's room with plywood partitions, leaving the daughter a pariah, alone in a cramped, dark space without windows and only a

Take a moment to pray for the
sick African mother who cannot
work and cannot feed her children.
Pray for relief from the physical
suffering and the emotional
helplessness she feels. Pray for her
children, that they will be fed,
clothed, and nurtured, even when
she may no longer be with them.

flimsy door opening into the alley. Laetitia must earn the pennies
to feed herself and her children by peddling beer, cigarettes, and
candy from a shopping cart in her room, when people are brave
enough to stop by her door. "Sometimes they buy, sometimes
not," she says. "That is how I'm surviving."

Her mother will not talk to her. "If you are not even accepted
by your own family," says Magwazi, the volunteer home-care
giver from Durban's Sinoziso project who visits Laetitia, "then
others will not accept you." When Laetitia ventures outdoors,
neighbors snub her, tough boys snatch her purse, children taunt
her. Her own kids are tired of the sickness and don't like to help
her anymore. "When I can't get up, they don't bring me food,"
she laments. One day local youths barged into her room, cursed
her as a witch and a whore, and beat her. When she told the
police, the youths returned, threatening to burn down the house.

But it is her mother's rejection that wounds Laetitia most. "She is hiding it about my brother," she cries. "Why will she do nothing for me?" Her hands pick restlessly at the quilt covering her paper-thin frame. "I know my mother will not bury me properly. I know she will not take care of my kids when I am gone."

Jabulani Syabusi would use his real name, but he needs to protect his brother. He teaches school in a red, dusty district of KwaZulu-Natal. People here know the disease is all around them, but no one speaks of it. He eyes the scattered huts that make up his little settlement on an arid bluff. "We can count twenty who died just here as far as we can see. I personally don't remember any family that told it was AIDS," he says. "They hide it if they do know."

Syabusi's own family is no different. His younger brother is also a teacher who has just come home from Durban too sick to work anymore. He says he has tuberculosis, but after six months the tablets he is taking have done nothing to cure him. Syabusi's wife Nomsange, a nurse, is concerned that her thirty-six-year-old brother-in-law may have something worse. Syabusi finally asked the doctor tending his brother what is wrong. The doctor said the information is confidential and will not tell him. Neither will his brother. "My brother is not brave enough to tell me," says Syabusi, as he stares sadly toward the house next door, where his only sibling lies ill. "And I am not brave enough to ask him."

Kennedy Fugewane, a cheerful, elderly volunteer counselor, sits in an empty U.S.-funded clinic that offers fast, pinprick blood tests in Francistown, Botswana, pondering how to break through the silence. This city suffers one of the world's highest infection rates, but people deny the disease because HIV is linked with sex. "We don't reveal anything," he says. "But people are so stigmatized even if they walk in the door." Africans feel they must keep private anything to do with sex. "If a man comes here, people will say he is running around," says Fugewane, though he acknowledges that men never do come. "If a woman comes, people will say she is loose. If anyone says they got HIV, they will be despised."

Pretoria University's Mary Crewe says, "It is presumed if you get AIDS, you have done something wrong." HIV labels you as living an immoral life. Embarrassment about sexuality looms more important than future health risks. "We have no language to talk candidly about sex," she says, "so we have no civil language to talk about AIDS." Volunteers like Fugewane try to reach out with fliers, workshops, youth meetings, and free condoms, but they are frustrated by a culture that values its dignity over saving lives. "People here don't have the courage to come forward and say, 'Let me know my HIV status,'" he sighs, "much less the courage to do something about it. Maybe one day . . ."

Doctors bow to social pressure and legal strictures not to record AIDS on death certificates. "I write TB or meningitis or diarrhea but never AIDS," says South Africa's Dr. Moll. "It's a public document, and families would hate it if anyone knew." Several years ago, doctors were barred even from recording compromised immunity or HIV status on a medical file; now they can record the results of blood tests for AIDS on patient charts to protect other health workers. Doctors like Moll have long agitated to apply the same openness to death certificates.

THE CHILD IN NO. 17

In crib No. 17 of the spartan but crowded children's ward at the Church of Scotland Hospital in KwaZulu-Natal, a tiny, staring child lies dying. She is three and has hardly known a day of good health. Now her skin wrinkles around her body like an oversize suit, and her twig-size bones can barely hold her vertical as nurses search for a vein to take blood. In the frail arms hooked up to transfusion tubes, her veins have collapsed. The nurses palpate a threadlike vessel on the child's forehead. She mews like a wounded animal as one tightens a rubber band around her head to raise the vein. Tears pour unnoticed from her mother's eyes as she watches the needle tap-tap at her daughter's temple. Each time the whimpering child lifts a wan hand to brush away the pain, her mother gently lowers it. Drop by drop, the nurses manage to collect 1 cc of blood in five minutes.

The child in crib No. 17 has had TB, oral thrush, chronic diarrhea, malnutrition, severe vomiting. The vial of blood reveals her real ailment, AIDS, but the disease is not listed on her chart, and her mother says she has no idea why her child is so ill. She breastfed her for two years, but once the little girl was weaned, she could not keep solid food down. For a long time, her mother thought something was wrong with the food. Now the child is afflicted with so many symptoms that her mother had to bring her to the hospital, from which sick babies rarely return.

She hopes, she prays her child will get better, and like all the mothers who stay with their children at the hospital, she tends to her lovingly, constantly changing filthy diapers, smoothing sheets, pressing a little nourishment between listless lips, trying to tease a smile from the vacant, staring face. Her husband works in Johannesburg, where he lives in a men's squatter camp. He comes home twice a year. She is twenty-five. She has heard of AIDS but does not know it is transmitted by sex, does not know if she or her husband has it. She is afraid this child will die soon, and she is afraid to have more babies. But she is afraid, too, to raise the subject with her husband. "He would not agree to that," she says shyly. "He would never agree to have no more babies."

Dr. Annick DeBaets, thirty-two, is a volunteer from Belgium. In the two years she has spent here in Tugela Ferry, she has learned all about how hard it is to break the cycle of HIV transmission from mother to infant. The door to this forty-eight–cot ward is literally a revolving one: Sick babies come in, receive

HIV/AIDS is "a threat that puts in the balance the future of nations," South African president Nelson Mandela said in an address to the World Economic Forum. "AIDS kills those on whom society relies to grow the crops, work in the mines and factories, run the schools and hospitals, and govern countries. . . . It creates new pockets of poverty when parents and breadwinners die and children leave school earlier to support the remaining children."

doses of rudimentary antibiotics, vitamins, food; go home for a week or a month; then come back as ill as ever. Most, she says, die in the first or second year. If she could just follow up with really intensive care, believes Dr. DeBaets, many of the wizened infants crowding three to a crib could live longer, healthier lives. "But it's very discouraging. We simply don't have the time, money, or facilities for anything but minimal care."

Much has been written about what South African Judge Edwin Cameron, himself HIV positive, calls his country's "grievous ineptitude" in the face of the burgeoning epidemic. Nowhere has that been more evident than in the government's failure to provide drugs that could prevent pregnant women from passing HIV to their babies. The government has said it can't afford the three-hundred-rand-per-dose, twenty-eight-dose regimen of AZT that neighboring nations like Botswana dole out, using funds and drugs from foreign donors. The late South African presidential spokesman Parks Mankahlana even suggested publicly that it was not cost effective to save these children when their mothers were already doomed to die: "We don't want a generation of orphans."

Yet these children—70,000 are born HIV positive in South Africa alone every year—could be protected from the disease for about $4 each with another simple, cheap drug called nevirapine. Until last month, the South African government steadfastly refused to license or finance the use of nevirapine, despite the manufacturer's promise to donate the drug for five years, claiming that its "toxic" side effects are not yet known. This spring, however, the drug will finally be distributed to leading public hospitals in the country, though only on a limited basis at first.

The mother at crib No. 17 is not concerned with potential side effects. She sits on the floor cradling her daughter, crooning over and over, "Get well, my child, get well." The baby stares back without blinking. "It's sad, so sad, so sad," the mother says. The child died three days later.

The children who are left when parents die only add another complex dimension to Africa's epidemic. At seventeen, Tsepho Phale has been head of an indigent household of three young boys in the dusty township of Monarch, outside Francistown, for two years. He never met his father, his mother died of AIDS, and the grieving children possess only a raw concrete shell of a house. The doorways have no doors; the window frames no glass. There is not a stick of furniture. The boys sleep on piled-up blankets, their few clothes dangling from nails. In the room that passes for a kitchen, two paraffin burners sit on the dirt floor alongside the month's food: four cabbages, a bag of oranges and one of potatoes, three sacks of flour, some yeast, two jars of oil, and two cartons of milk. Next to a dirty stack of plastic pans lies the mealy meal and rice that will provide their main sustenance for the month. A couple of bars of soap and two rolls of toilet paper also have to last the month. Tsepho has just brought these rations home from the social service center where the "orphan grants" are doled out.

Tsepho has been robbed of a childhood that was grim even before his mother fell sick. She supported the family by "buying and selling things," he says, but she never earned more than a pittance. When his middle brother was knocked down by a car and left physically and mentally disabled, Tsepho's mother used the insurance money to build this house, so she would have one thing of value to leave her children. As the walls went up, she fell sick. Tsepho had to nurse her, bathe her, attend to her bodily functions, try to feed her. Her one fear as she lay dying was that her rural relatives would try to steal the house. She wrote a letter bequeathing it to her sons and bade Tsepho hide it.

Do you or someone you know have an ailing grandparent who requires constant care? Consider if instead of a grandparent, it was your parent. Now think about what life would be like if you were the designated caregiver. This is the experience of many young people in Africa today.

As her body lay on the concrete floor awaiting burial, the relatives argued openly about how they would divide up the profits when they sold her dwelling. Tsepho gave the district commissioner's office the letter, preventing his mother's family from grabbing the house. Fine, said his relations; if you think you're a man, you look after your brothers. They have contributed nothing to the boys' welfare since. "It's as if we don't exist anymore either," says Tsepho. Now he struggles to keep house for the others, doing the cooking, cleaning, laundry, and shopping.

The boys look at the future with despair. "It is very bleak," says Tsepho, kicking aimlessly at a bare wall. He had to quit school, has no job, will probably never get one. "I've given up my dreams. I have no hope."

Orphans have traditionally been cared for the African way: Relatives absorb the children of the dead into their extended families. Some still try, but communities like Tsepho's are becoming saturated with orphans, and families can't afford to take on another kid, leaving thousands alone.

Now many must fend for themselves, struggling to survive. The trauma of losing parents is compounded by the burden of becoming a breadwinner. Most orphans sink into penury, drop out of school, suffer malnutrition, ostracism, psychic distress. Their makeshift households scramble to live on pitiful handouts—from overstretched relatives, a kind neighbor, a state grant—or they beg and steal in the streets. The orphans' present desperation forecloses a brighter future. "They hardly ever succeed in having a life," says Siphelile Kaseke, twenty-two, a counselor at an AIDS orphans' camp near Bulawayo. Without education, girls fall into prostitution, and older boys migrate illegally to South Africa, leaving the younger ones to go on the streets.

Every day spent in this part of Africa is acutely depressing: There is so little countervailing hope to all the stories of the dead and the doomed. "More than anywhere else in the world, AIDS in Africa was met with apathy," says Suzanne LeClerc-Madlala, a lecturer at the University of Natal. The consequences of the silence march on: Infection soars, stigma hardens, denial hastens death, and the chasm between knowledge and behavior widens. The present disaster could be dwarfed by the woes that loom if Africa's epidemic rages on. The human losses could wreck the region's frail economies, break down civil societies, and incite political instability.

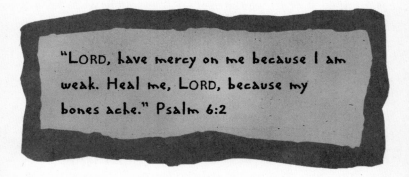

"LORD, have mercy on me because I am weak. Heal me, LORD, because my bones ache." Psalm 6:2

In the face of that, every day good people are doing good things. Like Dr. Moll, who uses his after-job time and his own fund raising to run an extensive volunteer home-care program in KwaZulu-Natal. And Busi Magwazi, who, along with dozens of others, tends the sick for nothing in the Durban-based Sinoziso project. And Patricia Bakwinya, who started her Shining Stars orphan care program in Francistown with her own zeal and no money, to help youngsters like Tsepho Phale. And countless individuals who give their time and devotion to ease southern Africa's plight.

But these efforts can help only thousands; they cannot turn the tide. The region is caught in a double bind. Without treatment, those with HIV will sicken and die; without prevention, the spread of infection cannot be checked. Southern Africa has no other means available to break the vicious cycle, except to change everyone's sexual behavior—and that isn't happening.

The essential missing ingredient is leadership. Neither the

countries of the region nor those of the wealthy world have been able or willing to provide it.

South Africa, comparatively well off, comparatively well educated, has blundered tragically for years. AIDS invaded just when apartheid ended, and a government absorbed in massive transition relegated the disease to a back page. An attempt at a national education campaign wasted millions on a farcical musical. The premature release of a local wonder drug ended in scandal when the drug turned out to be made of industrial solvent. Those fiascos left the government skittish about embracing expensive programs, inspiring a 1998 decision not to provide AZT to HIV-positive pregnant women. Zimbabwe, too, suffers savagely from feckless leadership. Even in Botswana, where the will to act is gathering strength, the resources to follow through have to come from foreign hands.

AIDS' grip here is so pervasive and so complex that all societies—theirs and ours—must rally round to break it. These countries are too poor to doctor themselves. The drugs that could begin to break the cycle will not be available here until global pharmaceutical companies find ways to provide them inexpensively. The health care systems required to prescribe and monitor complicated triple-cocktail regimens won't exist unless rich countries help foot the bill. If there is ever to be a vaccine, the West will have to finance its discovery and provide it to the poor. The cure for this epidemic is not national but international.

The deep silence that makes African leaders and societies want to deny the problem, the corruption and incompetence that render them helpless, is something the West cannot fix. But the fact that they are poor is not. The wealthy world must help with its zeal and its cash if southern Africa is ever to be freed of the AIDS plague.

Written by Johanna McGeary. From "Death Stalks a Continent" for Time, *copyright © by* Time.

Interview with John Reuben

JOHN REUBEN

 ood morning, John. Thanks for talking with us.
Good morning! Thanks for talking with me.

You're a hip-hop artist from Ohio. How did you get interested in the AIDS crisis in Africa?
I first heard about it from a guy at my label. He told me about the purpose of DATA and what it stands for. I felt like it was something I could really get behind.

So was there one moment when you realized that this was the cause you wanted to fight for, or was it a more gradual realization?
I realized from the beginning that this was something I wanted to get behind. However, the more I learned about it and understood the details, it was like I really had no choice but to support it. The AIDS crisis in Africa is too real and too big to ignore. As time has gone on, I have found that it's not something that I just want to display in a newsletter on my merchandise table, but it's something that I really want to get involved with.

DATA is an acronym for Debt, AIDS, Trade, Africa. Its purpose is to raise awareness about the crisis swamping Africa: unpayable debts, uncontrolled spread of AIDS, and trade rules that add to the problem of poverty.

There are a lot of issues that you could have picked to champion. In fact, your mom went through a church-based assistance program before you were born. Why did you pick this one?

I support a lot of causes and a lot of different things that deal with different issues and struggles people are going through. As far as how much time and energy you can devote, there is only so much you can do before you spread yourself too thin. The issue in Africa is something I can really support as an artist and really want to support. To be honest with you, I am just now getting more into it, and the more I find out, the more it breaks my heart.

What stories have you heard from Africa? Help us get a mental picture of the devastation.

There are more orphans there than there is room in the orphanages. There are people dying and no medical supplies to treat them. I remember seeing video footage from a friend who went over to Africa on a mission trip. One thing in particular that broke my heart was seeing this kid crying his eyes out and praying for the kids in his orphanage. Here he was in the same exact situation they were in, and yet he was crying out and praying for them.

Why do you want your listeners to care about this?

I would hope that people who listen to my music and especially those who call themselves believers would step out of their boundaries. I would hope that the music I put out—and if you mean by my listeners people that listen to my music and get something out of it—that those people would get more out of it than just entertainment. I hope my listeners would be people who genuinely care about things outside their comfort zone, and that they would see a higher purpose. I hope that people—nonbelievers and especially believers—could actually step outside their comfort zones and put themselves in someone else's shoes and do something to help.

What can they really do? I mean, they're at home in Middle America. How can they make a difference?

Awareness and acknowledgment are the biggest things first of all. In general, this means bringing awareness to others and being aware yourself. Even if it just means broadening the perspective of people in your communities and schools by telling them about this situation, you are doing something practical to help. Also, not to sound cliché, but I believe that prayer works and we need to be praying about this.

> Do a Web search using keywords *AIDS* and *Africa*. Visit at least five sites and educate yourself on the medical, political, financial, and psychological issues of this growing pandemic.

What's your hope for Africa?

This thing is so big it's hard to answer that. Obviously I would love to see the continent healed and prospering. But right now, I would just like to see people around the world doing their part to help. The reality is that we can do something, and we can encourage the leaders of this nation and others to do something.

Where do you see Africa in five, ten years? Will any of this make a difference?

A lot of small steps can lead to huge change. To be honest with you, whether or not Africa is in the same place five to ten years from now, we should still be doing something because there are people in need, and we need to be doing something to help. However, I do believe that what we are doing today is going to make a difference, and Africa is going to be in a lot better place five to ten years from now.

Thanks so much for your time, John. Is there anything else you wanted to say?

Thank you. If anyone wants more information about DATA or the situation in Africa, please visit the official Website at www.datadata.org.

Interview for Mission: Africa, *copyright © 2003 by John Reuben.*

Hope for the Hopeless

MARGARET BECKER

I guess what stood out to me when I first arrived in the Mathari Valley was the absolute hopelessness. Everywhere, the brown dirt was littered with cardboard and tin.

The windows of our UN SUV were closed, their panes so hot we couldn't touch them. It was at least 100 degrees outside. Reality seemed skewed as we passed the desperate sights. It was as if we were watching a television show, where the windows were television screens. It was all in front of us, but in some odd way we were not entirely responsive to it, because we were passing through. We would go to a hotel that night in the city. We would go home at the end of the week. *We* only had to look— only for a little while.

We didn't even have to get out of the car if we didn't want to.

We drove for what seemed like a half-hour at least, through the tiny dirt roads lined with people and lean-tos. People sitting in the dirt, watching us pass in our white vehicle, watching with no expression. Neither interest nor disdain. Nothingness.

I was in Kenya with an organization that has been in the business of offering relief to the world for fifty years, through education and intervention: World Vision.

We were to have a police escort this morning, but fires broke out in this squatter settlement, and all the officials were battling it. Police are necessary to prevent kidnappings of foreigners. We were told to stay close together and be aware of our surroundings.

Mile upon mile of families, some twelve and thirteen people, huddled on small clusters of dirt that they considered "theirs." True squatters, someone was designated to remain at all times, otherwise others would come and assume ownership. Some of the luckier among the people had corrugated steel panels that were leaned against one another to create a makeshift tent or wall. The toilet for all was a small gully the size of a gutter that was etched into the middle of the dirt road.

I watched it pass from the relative comfort of the truck. I knew what I was seeing, but it didn't penetrate, even though I'd braced myself for the reality of it all before I ever arrived in Africa. World Vision warned me of what I might see: extreme poverty, desperate sickness, deformities caused by simple things like zinc deficiencies, so many hopeless situations. They told me, but I still wasn't prepared. How could I be? There is no reference here in my world. We have poverty but for the most part not like this.

All week long we saw how the tiniest of interventions, like educating adults on the necessity of clean water, had changed the settlement for the better, saving lives from inane deaths caused by diarrhea.

At one project, a simple education on how to sew saved sixty women a year from prostitution—one of the more commonplace occupations for women in the Third World. But with organizations like World Vision, these Kenyan ladies were offered alternatives. I hovered in their little workshop, happy for the hope I felt. These women had a plan. They had simple resources, and their whole lives would be different now—in a better way. A future for these families, a future that we would despise according to our standards but that was more than they could have ever hoped for.

> The Land and Agricultural Policy Centre (LAPC) estimates that over 50 percent of rural households in South Africa are headed by women. For some, this is because their spouses are away, working in urban areas as migrant laborers. Others have lost their husbands to disease. These women are solely responsible for caring for children and keeping the family intact with very scant resources.

Two days into the visit we went to the trash piles, the place where Nairobi dumps all of its urban garbage. The stench was overwhelming, burning the eyes. Hills upon hills of garbage heaps with, of all things, people perched atop them. Babies without shoes or clothing, barely able to walk, sifting through the piles for anything with which they can barter. A piece of wire that can be twisted to make a bracelet. A half-eaten meal—anything. Our Kenyan guide explained the lack of adults on the pile.

"The hospital puts its trash here, too. They do not dispose of their used utensils in any special way; they just toss them here. Of course you know about our problem with AIDS. These people here on the trash actually live there. Some never come down for their entire lives because if they leave, someone will take their place.

"The adults and the babies are mostly AIDS infected, from pricking themselves on the needles left over from the hospital, and then—as adults will do—having sexual intercourse."

We stared. A baby forced his tiny hand into a smoldering opening in the heap about thirty feet up.

The guide spanned the vista, jaw set deep in thought. He turned to us finally and simply said, "AIDS is our biggest problem."

The last place we stopped on our tour was the AIDS Orphan Day Program. We walked into the tiny mud building to a group of children all wearing white T-shirts with the words "AIDS Orphan" printed on the front in English.

The fact that they wore anything declaring that they were connected to AIDS was shocking. In America, we've been so long averse to even discussing it, hiding behind the false veil of a "lifestyle" connection. To say *AIDS* was akin to saying *homosexual*. People felt free of any responsibility because it wasn't their problem. They led good lives.

Yet here, from infants to adolescents, were children, wearing these shirts that plainly spoke of their situation.

There was no shame. They had a disease. It was a tragic disease that would eventually kill them. That was it.

According to a report entitled "No Excuses," published by Christian Aid (May 2001), by 2010 an estimated 43 million children will be orphaned by AIDS.

Our guide explained how the parents and their aunts and uncles had died of AIDS. It is almost wiping out an entire generation, leaving only the very young and the very old.

Grandparents who had long since raised their children—most times with great difficulty, now were forced to reenter the fight to survive, to provide for their children's children. Some of them began with six children of their own. Now they were caring for multitudes—in some cases, more than twenty—with no house, no food, no source of income.

There are more than 13 million of these children now. *Thirteen million.*

A small boy came up to me as I considered these things. He reached his arms out to me, and I picked him up.

There we were, two living, breathing people, looking into one another's eyes. His shy smile convicted me and challenged me to forget everything I thought I knew about our world and how it works, about what is fair and not fair, about social stigmas and prejudices. It challenged me to find a way—*make* a way—to help the people I come in contact with *see him.* Just one person who will die a terrible death very soon, just one small boy who smiles, because he has a T-shirt and some food and people who will hold him from time to time.

I couldn't retreat behind the glass any longer. Standing in a continent where some rates of infection are as high as 35 percent—one-third of the population in some countries.

I thought of the national study done by World Vision that showed how Christians feel about this issue and mourned. I vowed that I would not be one of the 61 percent who will not help overseas AIDS prevention and education programs. I *wouldn't* be one of the 54 percent who openly admit that they will do nothing to help. I did not have the luxury of turning a blind eye, because I held a boy in my arms. Just a boy. *Only* a boy.

A boy whose parents didn't know that unprotected sex was

deadly. A boy whose mother or father received tainted blood, or stepped on a needle—just *people* living out *human lives,* with all the dramatic and mundane situations that we *all* face.

World Vision has helped me to help. They've been intervening in the African AIDS crisis since 1990. They couldn't ignore it then, when the rest of Christian America could. And now, as the epidemic threatens to affect our lives in every area from our economy to our health, I hope that we will all rise to the challenge—the way Jesus himself would.

I hope we get out of the car, walk in the unlovely places, and begin picking people up one by one, changing the world one person at a time.

And I pray that we do it all in the name of the greatest hope, our merciful, loving God, Jesus Christ.

Written for The aWAKE Project, *copyright © 2002 by Margaret Becker.*

Interview with Peter Furler

THE NEWSBOYS

 ood afternoon, Peter. How are you?
Good, thanks.

We're here to talk about AIDS in Africa. How did you first find out about the AIDS crisis?
I found out about the AIDS emergency through people who cared what the Scripture said we are to do for the poor and needy.

There are so many causes to support. What makes AIDS in Africa so important to you?
AIDS is important to me because it's important to God. God hates disease; his only Son gave his blood to wash us clean of the virus that not only kills the body but also kills the soul.

It's difficult to believe one can make any difference in an unknown, distant continent with such an enormous problem.
Sometimes it can be, but that's what an enemy would want us to believe. Anything that stops us from helping an orphan or a widow, a brother or a sister—there's a good chance it is an enemy of theirs and ours.

> By narrowly viewing AIDS as a disease affecting only drug users and homosexuals, how have some Christians actually worsened the problem, rather than helped? What can you do to change the attitudes of those around you?

We can care all we want, but in the end, are we really making a tangible difference?

Matthew 25 says that whatever we do to the face of Africa we do to the face of Jesus. That's real enough for me.

You're in a Christian band. Should Christians specifically be making a difference?

We should be like the Good Samaritan, not like the Priest or Levite who passed the afflicted by.

Do you have any advice for your fans?

Ask God to give us all wisdom and guidance in ways to help Africa.

What do you wish people understood about AIDS?

I don't believe that God created this world with AIDS in it. He created it beautiful. The world is groaning and waiting for restoration. This is a disease that attacks everyone, everywhere. The nice guy, the mother and child who didn't deserve it. I've learned that through the grace of God, AIDS might be an opportunity for God to be glorified. God didn't create AIDS. It's the Fall. The remedy is the blood of Christ that washed us so that we could become little Christs.

How have the Newsboys helped Africa so far, and what plans do you guys have for the future?

At the moment, at the top of our heads it's to do what we're good at, being very resourceful. We're a band that builds portable arenas to play in. We want to be in Africa a few times a year. We're most useful when we're building something. Education—knowing and sharing—is also a priority.

Do you have any other thoughts, comments regarding Africa's AIDS crisis?

Just that it would never be a mistake to help. If someone is scared about making a bad decision, this is not one.

Interview for Mission: Africa, *copyright © 2003 by Peter Furler.*

The Effect of AIDS on the Conscience, Heart, and Mind

MICHAEL TAIT

I would imagine that to most people AIDS seems very distant, very hard to understand. If it hasn't affected someone close to us, we feel naively immune to the disease. When my sister, Sharon, contracted the disease, it took her a long time before she told anyone. I imagine she felt shame and fear at our response. Actually, I think she might have told my girlfriend first. That was early in 1995; in June of 1996 she passed away.

I never really gave much thought to AIDS—it hadn't become personal to me yet. That all changed when Sharon told us she had HIV and it had progressed to full-blown AIDS. That was hard—it triggered all sorts of fears in me. I remember thinking to myself, *If I kiss her, will I get it? What if she starts bleeding; should I help her?*

Should I wear gloves? If I somehow got her saliva on me, would the disease spread to me? Because I didn't know enough about AIDS, fear was my first reaction. I remember feeling almost like Sharon had become a leper. When AIDS touches your family, it changes your perspective. It changed our family. It changed my life.

When she passed, she left two beautiful girls behind. It was, and still is, very difficult. You don't get over the effect of AIDS. You move beyond and hopefully come out on the other side with the

> ## Have you ever personally known some-one with AIDS?

determination to do your part to help end this disease. As Michael Tait, brother and uncle, I need to find my individual part. As part of the church, I need to share our story and help the church take an active part in reaching out to those affected. If you haven't been affected personally, you are blessed. That does not mean you have the privilege to ignore the heartbreak that AIDS has brought to those around the world. Africa is in an extreme situation. We need to be concerned and have compassion for those people. We need to find a way as the body of Christ to be involved.

People who have this disease need our love more than ever. Don't run from people with AIDS. We need to fight the fear to ostracize them because of the disease. We need to love these people as Christ loves these people. Christ loved and reached out to the Samaritan woman at the well—she was very different from him. We need to ask for his love to reach out to the suffering and comfort them in what may be their last days on earth.

Written for The aWAKE Project, *copyright © 2002 by Michael Tait.*

Jogging Past the AIDS Clinic

PHILIP YANCEY

S ome of my best "reading" time occurs as I jog along Chicago's lakefront, outfitted with Walkman and head-phones, listening to books recorded on cassette tape. One winter the city's dingy streets and rat-gray skies formed a perfect back-drop for the book I had selected: Daniel Defoe's *A Journal of the Plague Year*. In meticulous, matter-of-fact prose, he describes the bubonic plague that afflicted London in 1665.

In the account (which renders history in the form of realistic fiction), Defoe wanders the streets of a ghost city. Over 200,000 people have fled London, and those who remain barricade them-selves indoors, terrified of human contact. On main thorough-fares, where steady streams of people once trod, new grass grows. "Sorrow and sadness sat upon every face," says Defoe. At the peak of the plague, fifteen hundred to seventeen hundred people died each day, their bodies collected nightly for burial in cavernous open pits. The book describes gruesome scenes: dead children locked in the permanent grip of their parents' rigor mortis, live babies sucking in vain at the breasts of just-dead mothers.

As I listened, Defoe's account took on particular poignancy in view of a modern-day plague. My wife and I live in a neighborhood populated by many gays and not a few drug users. I could not avoid reflecting on the parallels between Defoe's time and our own as I jogged past a clinic for AIDS patients and dodged lamp-posts plastered with "AIDS Benefit" posters. Compared with the Great Plague, the AIDS epidemic has afflicted a much smaller proportion of the population, but it has stirred up a remarkably similar response of hysteria.

In Defoe's day, it seemed that God's molten wrath was being poured out on the entire planet. Two bright comets appeared in the sky each night—sure signs, said some, of God's hand behind the plague. Wild-eyed prophets roamed the streets, one echoing Jonah with his cry, "Yet forty days and London shall be destroyed!" Another walked around naked, balancing a pan of burning charcoal on his head to symbolize God's judgment. Still another naked prophet dolefully repeated the same phrase all day long: "Oh, the great and dreadful God! Oh, the great and dreadful God . . ."

We have our modern version of these prophets. Most are well clothed, however, and they tend to narrow the focal point of God's judgment down to one particular group, the homosexuals, who are disproportionately represented among AIDS sufferers in the U.S. In some circles I can almost detect a sigh of relief, a satisfaction that at last "they are getting what they deserve." Former Surgeon General C. Everett Koop, an evangelical Christian, received boxes full of hate mail whenever he dared to suggest otherwise.

The AIDS crisis taps into a mysterious yearning among human beings, a deep-rooted desire that suffering ought to be tied to behavior. I have a book on my shelf, *Theories of Illness,* that surveys 139 tribal groups from around the world; all but four of them perceive illness as a sign of God's (or the gods') disapproval. The author notes that the few who doubt such doctrine probably changed their beliefs after prolonged contact with modern civilization.

From the 1970s until 1982, when the United States formally named the disease and began tracking cases of AIDS, there were 121 deaths attributed to an elusive "Gay Cancer," also called GRID (Gay-Related Immune Deficiency). By 2000, an estimated 2.8 million people had died from AIDS.

Virtually alone among all civilizations in history, our modern, secular one questions whether God plays a direct role in such human events as plagues and natural catastrophes. (Even we have our doubts: Insurance policies specify certain "acts of God.") We are confused. Did God single out one town in the Southeast to be leveled by a tornado as a message of judgment? Does he withhold rains from Africa as a sign of his displeasure? No one knows for sure. But AIDS—ah, there's a different story. Beyond dispute, the likelihood of AIDS transmission increases among those who engage in promiscuous sex or share dirty needles.

For some Christians, AIDS seems to satisfy at last the longing for a precise connection between behavior and suffering-as-punishment. In a general sense, the connection has been established—in the same way that smoking increases risk of cancer, obesity increases risk of heart disease, and heterosexual promiscuity increases risk of venereal disease. The natural consequences of such behavior include, in many cases, physical suffering; scientists recognize this fact and advertise it widely. But the lurking question remains: Did God send AIDS as a specific, targeted punishment?

Other Christians are not so sure. They see a grave danger in playing God, or even interpreting history on his behalf. Like Job's friends, we can too easily come across as cranky or smug, not prophetic. "Vengeance is mine," God said, and whenever we mortals try to appropriate his vengeance, we tread on dangerous ground. Judgment without love makes enemies, not converts. Among the gays in my neighborhood, Christians' statements about the AIDS crisis have done little to encourage reconciliation.

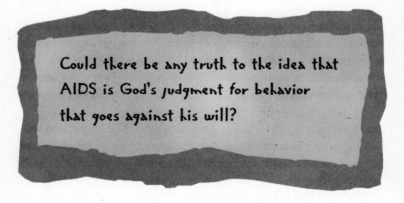

Could there be any truth to the idea that AIDS is God's judgment for behavior that goes against his will?

Even the apparent cause-and-effect tie to behavior in AIDS raises troubling questions. What of "innocent" sufferers, such as the babies born to infected mothers or those who received the virus in a blood transfusion? Are they tokens of God's judgment? And if a cure is suddenly found—will that signify an end to God's punishment? Theologians in Europe expostulated for *four centuries* about God's message in the Great Plague; but it took only a little rat poison to silence all those anguished questions.

Reflecting on these two plagues, the scourge of the buboes

that killed off a third of humanity and the modern scourge with its kindred hysteria, I find myself turning to an incident from Jesus' life recorded in Luke 13:2–5 (NIV). When some people asked him about a contemporary tragedy, here is how he responded:

> 'Do you think that these Galileans were worse sinners than all the other Galileans because they suffered this way? I tell you, no! But unless you repent, you too will all perish. Or those eighteen who died when the tower in Siloam fell on them—do you think they were more guilty than all the others living in Jerusalem? I tell you, no! But unless you repent, you too will all perish.'

Then Jesus followed up with a parable about God's restraining mercy. He seems to imply that we "bystanders" of catastrophe have as much to learn from the event as do the sufferers themselves. What should a plague teach us? Humility, for one thing. And gratitude that God has so far withheld the judgment all of us deserve. And compassion, the compassion that Jesus displayed to all who mourn and suffer. Finally, catastrophe joins together victim and bystander in a common call to repentance by abruptly reminding us of the brevity of life. It warns us to make ourselves ready in case we are the next victim of a falling tower—or an AIDS virus.

I have yet to find any support in the Bible for an attitude of smugness: *Ah, they deserve their punishment; watch them squirm.* Indeed, the message of a plague seems directed to survivors as much as to the afflicted. I guess AIDS holds as much meaning for those of us who jog past the clinics as for those who suffer inside.

Interview with The Benjamin Gate

THE BENJAMIN GATE

ood evening, guys. How are you?
Good, thanks.

Well, we're here to speak about the AIDS crisis in Africa, your home continent. There are so many worthwhile causes in the world today to support. Why is Africa's AIDS crisis so important?

Costa: It's a disease that's killing off our world. Africa is the first to suffer. Who knows what country could be next.

Mac: Yes, it's a growing crisis that's affecting people who can't help themselves. Personally, it directly affects my family and friends who live in a country that's about to be plagued with death.

Chris: The African AIDS crisis is a problem that goes largely unnoticed and is spreading at an alarming rate. The AIDS crisis will kill nations of people, a lot of whom are uneducated on the subject of AIDS.

Why should Christians, specifically, become involved in helping Africa with its AIDS crisis?

> We've all heard it said that education
> is the key weapon in fighting AIDS.
> Learn five new facts about HIV/AIDS
> (how it is spread, treatment options,
> how many people are affected, etc.) and
> share them with at least three friends.

Nick: To be an example to the world—to make a real difference in this world by helping our fellowman and showing unconditional love.

Adrienne: There are a lot of reasons. The Bible calls us to love our neighbors as we love ourselves. We are also called to serve each other and reach out and help those in need.

Chris: Yes, it is a foundation of Christianity to help fellow human beings, to reach out in any way, whether it's educating or taking care of practical needs.

How can Christians become practically involved in helping?

Nick: They can visit a hospital with an AIDS ward in their community and meet some AIDS patients—get to know them and their feelings. Ask them what needs to be done.

Adrienne: And by raising funds and awareness, and challenging our leaders and each other to be more effective. Also by holding meetings to encourage each other to be more involved, and to reach out to those in need.

Chris: Christians can help by having people who can actually be there in the field helping, and those who can't be there can pray and help with collecting resources.

> Get involved! Contact your local hospice or AIDS support group and find out how you can help those in your own community who are suffering with the disease.

What personal experience of the AIDS crisis in your home country, South Africa, made it the most real to you?

Adrienne: I've known a few people who've been infected by the virus through blood transfusion. The AIDS crisis in Africa is so prevalent you almost become used to it. I think for me the reality hit home when I realized how many people are suffering and have died from it. Also, seeing firsthand the poverty and life status of people in Africa.

Nick: I visited AIDS patients, and it was a wake-up call and a shock. Besides being deeply moved and saddened, it made me realize how many people are not aware of the seriousness of this virus.

Chris: A good friend had a blood transfusion and got infected with the HIV virus. Also, casual workers that family members worked with have died of AIDS.

How has The Benjamin Gate helped Africa in a practical way so far?

Adrienne: We've tried to create awareness through our interviews, and we have sign-up sheets at our merchandise booth where people can receive e-mails and information. We've been involved in some hospital visits in South Africa.

What preparation tips would you give to Christians going to Africa to assist with the AIDS crisis?

Nick: Be educated and prepare your heart to unconditionally love your brother. Awareness and education are the tools to battle the further spread of this crisis.

Adrienne: Be prepared to work hard and be patient. I'm not sure how much preparation you can give a person when they will meet people who are dying. Be informed about the disease. Communicate and find out what people need. Let the beautiful spirit of Africa and its people capture your heart, and act.

Chris: Pray for patience and love.

Interview for Mission: Africa, *copyright © 2003 by The Benjamin Gate.*

The Presence and Promise of the Kingdom

SARAH MASEN

I hope that our hearts are ready for more as this new millennium begins. I pray that the church will move their ideas and dreams and buildings and people better under the lordship of Christ. That we would be willing to find out what this means, so we can live in the presence and the promise of the kingdom—what N. T. Wright calls the "double advent"—the understanding that the kingdom *has* come in Jesus, and his upside-down kind of love that is extended to our enemies and requires leaders to be servants, and the hope/belief/promise that his kingdom *is* coming. I hope that the church will take seriously its possible role in ushering in this kingdom—third way—ultimate alternative lifestyle that Jesus lived and died representing.

This to me means the church would be taking a more active role in feeding and caring for the poor (this includes the spiritually empty as well as the immediately hungry); taking care of the wiser ones who have a few years on us (the elderly), the widows and orphans (single mothers and children whose parents have emotionally checked out), and victims of war and violence (the church can be a powerful opponent to violence under the faith and sacrifice of pacifism; see Walter Wink or John Howard

Yoder); supporting Jubilee 2000 (the practice of extending mercy to countries in great need of debt cancellation); and becoming opponents of the death penalty (perhaps this means more involvement in the lives of prisoners and a great desire to see real forgiveness extended and embraced by those who have made decisions for fear and against life).

The church can be a place known for its compassion and convictions. Orthodox, Catholic, and Protestant. The bride of Christ is supposed to be representative of the eternal kind of life—*now*. And why not? We have the mind of Christ, the reality and history of his death's and his life's impact on the world, and we have his Father's help and unique love for each of us as individuals. My hope for the church in the new millennium is that we won't forget God's present and radically humanitarian way under the sleeping potion of "being realistic," but that we would change current systems and "powers" of selfishness and fear. It can be done.

Like Abraham, we can hope—even against hope—for his Way to come.

JARS OF CLAY

 ood afternoon, Dan. Thanks for talking with us today.
Thank you.

Your band, Jars of Clay, has been a real leader in the fight against AIDS in Africa. What has propelled you to become passionate about this issue?

It started a few years ago when I had a surprise guest over for Thanksgiving dinner. A man from Rwanda who had recently come to the U.S. seeking political asylum. He was preaching reconciliation between the Hutu and the Tutsi tribes and was flagged to be assassinated. So he fled to the U.S. I spent the next two years working alongside other people in the community to get his family over. He was my first introduction to Africa. My eyes had been opened, and more meetings and divine appointments came soon after. I began to read a book about the persecution of Christians in Sudan, and then ended up at a dinner with the director of the National Day of Prayer for the Persecuted Church. God was connecting me to something I had never even considered until that year.

From that point, it has been a steady awakening to the continent of Africa. In 2001, World Vision came to us and asked if we would consider being a bridge between the church and the HIV/AIDS crisis in Africa. Because of the negative stigma attached to HIV/AIDS and its close ties to the homosexual community, the church has played only a cursory role in helping people with AIDS, so World Vision asked us to speak about it. I began to read statistics and listen to stories and immerse myself in all that this emergency would allow. Then came DATA and meeting with Bono to hear his heart about the issue. Finally, I took a trip myself to connect my heart to this issue my mind was engaged in.

DATA—you're referring to Debt, AIDS, Trade, Africa—the organization Bono has started to address the issues relating to this crisis in Africa.

Right. Bono came over to Nashville this last winter and spoke to a group of musicians about the work he's doing to fight AIDS in Africa. It was an amazing time.

You just recently traveled with World Vision and an organization based here in Franklin, Tennessee, called African Leadership to Africa. What did you experience while you were there?

I went to three different countries, Malawi, Zimbabwe, and South Africa. It was an amazing experience for a number of reasons. African Leadership and World Vision are two very different organizations with different ways of impacting a community. African Leadership started as a pastoral training organization but since has supplemented the training with vocational skills training and food distribution as well as recent support for medical facilities in a few communities. They have a much more personal approach to community development. I was able to experience food distribution at a very powerful church community level, as well as a mass food dispersal with World Vision. I was able to see how important these programs are that become part of a community. The HIV/AIDS clinics and support groups have so much negative stigma to fight through that you have to build trust in a community in order to be effective. I saw very, very effective community development.

Do you plan to go back anytime soon?

My hope is to return soon. I know that the majority of my work on this issue will take place in the U.S. as I raise awareness and help support medical facilities through Blood: Water Mission. But I know that to keep my heart connected, I will need and want to go and spend time with the people of Africa.

Blood: Water Mission is the foundation you've started, right? Where can people go to find out more about that organization?

They can check out our Website: www.jarsofclay.com.

How has your interest in Africa affected your music?

As any strong life experience opens up a floodgate of emotions, this experience has done this. In a situation like this, the music has not really changed as much as the reason for playing has changed. I see the need to have a platform to speak about this issue. Music has afforded me the ability to speak to lots of people and to dream big about the kinds of creative projects I can start to raise awareness and support for Africa.

You're a hero to tons of people out there who love your music. Do you have any heroes who have inspired you to help other people?

I suppose I am always inspired by the hymn writers of the past. Their stories are always ones of grace coming in and changing their hearts. I love what Bono is doing. I recently celebrated my thirtieth birthday, and part of the experience was having an evening gathering of the five men who have mentored me over the past ten years. These men are my heroes. They are men who have been changed by the gospel, men who are humble and genuine.

Dan, from what I've seen, the situation in Africa seems hopeless at times. What keeps you passionate about continuing to fight when things look so desperate?

I have come to understand that distance is the enemy of Africa. When we look at this issue, we only see it from a world-map perspective. The statistics are all huge, overwhelming numbers; the death toll is too large to comprehend; the orphan situation is reaching to astronomical rates; but for me, when I dare get closer, I find the hope to keep working.

It is in the testimony of a single caregiver, working to get food to late-stage AIDS patients, or the women of a village taking on the burden of loving well the orphans in their own community. You have to get close to it to see the hope. It is there. And it is worth searching for.

How do you find peace in such troubling work?

The Scripture Isaiah 58:6–12. There is peace in knowing that this is God's work for me. This is God's work for all of us. There is something exciting in knowing that when I help the orphans and the sick, I am helping Jesus Christ. What more do we need to know?

What would you say to your fans who want to get involved and take the next step to do something about Africa's plight?

I think there are so many ways to be involved. *The aWAKE Project* is a wonderful book with a large list of organizations to come alongside. Jars of Clay is starting the Blood: Water Mission, a foundation with a primary focus of supporting grass-roots medical facilities in their distribution of medicines preventing HIV / AIDS from spreading to children during the birthing process.

Writing papers and speaking about the issue is free . . . and a great way to build support in an individual community. There is so much to do.

Thanks so much for your time.

Thank you.

Copyright © 2003 by Dan Haseltine.

Africa—It's Personal

CHARLIE PEACOCK

It was the Fourth of July, Independence Day—the first for the United States since 9/11. I took a seat at the desk in the recording studio and reached up and turned on the television to CNN. I'd come in to retrieve my journal for a little morning writing, and while close by, I surrendered to the temptation to check my e-mail. Glancing at the television, I could see the president speaking from a podium, framed by veterans of war, fleshy symbols of freedom's fight. I looked down at my laptop where two messages had popped up, both urgent.

The first was in regard to friend and colleague Grant Cunningham, who'd fallen and suffered a head injury while playing soccer. The message urged all who received it to "please pray." I shut off CNN and immediately began talking to God about what I trusted was a matter of mutual concern—our friend Grant. Next, I printed out the e-mail to give to my wife, Andi, so that she would talk with God about it as well.

The second e-mail was in regard to the ongoing and urgent crisis in Africa, specifically poverty and the deadly AIDS virus. Though the first e-mail might have appeared to be more personal, the second was no less.

As a student-follower of Jesus and the ways of God, I'm committed to having my understanding of *personal* undergo a lifelong incremental transformation. What's personal to God is step-by-step becoming personal to me as well. This is as it should be, given that God gave stewardship of his personal creativity to the human family.

The e-mail regarding Africa contained a link to an article on the Christian music community's involvement with U2's Bono and an organization called DATA, a dual acronym for stopping the crises of **D**ebt, **A**IDS, and **T**rade in Africa, in return for **D**emocracy, **A**ccountability, and **T**ransparency in Africa. Several people in our Nashville tribe (and beyond) have gathered together to help DATA tell the story of Africa's brokenness and need. The e-mail updated me on our progress and pointed me to a second link, an interview with Bono on the subject of DATA and Africa, in which he assured the interviewer that the world would be hearing from the sleeping giant that is the church.

I believed him (and still do). I wanted to shout "Amen!" and cue Al Green for a chorus or two. Judging by his actions in recent years, one could surmise that Bono has been doing a lot of talking with God about matters of mutual concern. He has been taking things like the care of widows and orphans very personally, as anyone should who claims to stumble after Jesus. The book of James reminds readers that the religion God accepts as pure and good is the care of orphans and widows in their distress (like those in Africa), and keeping oneself from being polluted by the world's ways of being and doing (like by caring less about your comfortable Western lifestyle and more about your dying neighbor across the ocean).

The usually cranky prophet Jeremiah tied one's knowledge of God to this very idea when he spoke of the good King Josiah: "'He defended the cause of the poor and needy, and so all went well. Is that not what it means to know me?' declares the Lord."[1]

Yet it's not just the poor and needy widows and orphans of Africa that have Bono speaking like the preacher of a congregation you'd actually like to join. I'm also quite sure this DATA idea is more than a pontificating rock star's grand gesture. From where I stand, it looks to me like real care and concern for the creativity of God overall—widows and orphans included, or especially. He's championing the summation of the Jewish law—love of God and neighbor—as well as the caretaking role given to the human family in the beginning. If you take all of life personally, as Jesus did, then the shape and territory of love expand further than you or I can imagine. Nevertheless, most of us can find Africa on the map.

Bono's passion for Africa (God's creativity in need of love and care), has bumped into us here in Music City. The collision woke more than a few sleepy musicians, myself included. Every day more and more music folk are being urged by the Spirit to tell the story of Africa and the story of the only good response, the God response. The one by which the image of God in humankind, made alive by the breath of God, cares for what God loves, his creation. It's the response by which men and women act congruently with the way they're made, and as a result, actually look like what they are—God's direct representatives here on earth.

Bono referred to the church as a "sleeping giant." What does this phrase mean? Do you feel that it is an accurate representation of the Christian community?

The wind of the Spirit is moving through the air. People are tuning in to the right channels. You can hear the very personal problem of Africa cutting through the distortion and racket of *me* and *mine*. The light is opening sleepy eyes. Distant concerns are coming near. Willing hearts and hands are bringing them even closer. Africa—God's creativity, filled with people made in his image, poor and needy.

Here's the action point: Talk to God and to each other about this important matter of mutual concern. Tell the story, and let people know through word and deed that you are taking it personally. This is the way of Jesus.

Written for The aWAKE Project, *copyright © 2002 by Charlie Peacock.*

1. Jeremiah 22:16 NIV

Indifferent Christians and the African Crisis

TONY CAMPOLO

I need not go into the agony that Africa is enduring under the impact of the AIDS epidemic. I wish you could see what I saw with my own eyes as I visited South Africa and Zimbabwe. The suffering I witnessed led me to get together the resources to start a program for the orphans of those who have died from AIDS. You meet them almost everywhere you go in those countries. Many of these children have AIDS themselves. Our program is designed to provide them with some loving care and sustenance. No child should be abandoned to the streets, covered with the body sores that accompany AIDS. No child should die alone without knowing that he or she is loved.

> "He will not forget the cries of those who suffer." Psalm 9:12

The social impact of AIDS is horrendous. In two of the schools I visited, there was a shortage of teachers because several of those who had held teaching positions had been victimized by the disease and were gone. I learned that schools throughout Africa are enduring this same loss of crucial personnel. The very people whom Africa needs to emerge out of economic privation are being liquidated by this dreaded disease.

I believe that too often the Christian response to the AIDS epidemic has been abominable. In many instances there is a tendency to write off those who are suffering from AIDS on the grounds that this disease is some kind of punishment from God meted out to those who have been sexually promiscuous. The logic behind such a conclusion is beyond my comprehension. Consider the fact that a huge number of those who are HIV positive are women who have been infected, not because of any immoral behavior on their part, but because their husbands gave them the disease. Are they to be condemned and ignored because of what their husbands have done? And what about the children who are infected? Children constitute a significant proportion of

Consider the parallel of AIDS and leprosy. Compare how people responded in biblical times to leprosy with how the modern world views AIDS. How did Jesus respond to those suffering from leprosy?

those who are facing the possibility of AIDS-related death through no fault of their own.

The Church must recognize that AIDS very much parallels the disease of leprosy that we read about in the New Testament. In biblical times, those who had leprosy were deemed spiritually unclean, and others would not get near them or touch them for fear of contamination that would be both physically harmful and spiritually defiling. Leprosy was seen to have a spiritual dimension to it, and those who had the disease were looked upon as being especially cursed by God. Given those realities about people who had leprosy back then, it is easy to understand why comparisons can be made with those who are infected by AIDS in our contemporary world.

It is important for us to note that Jesus had a special spot in his heart for the lepers. He embraced them. He touched them. He reached out to them in love. All of this was contrary to the legalistic pietism of religious leaders in his day. Jesus' condemnation of such religionists was harsh. He always reached out to the lepers to make them whole, in spite of the fact that touching them would render him ceremoniously unclean to the custodians of the temple religion.

The Jesus whom we find in Scripture calls upon us to look for him in the eyes of the poor and the oppressed. He tells us in Matthew 25 that what we do "to the least of them" we do to him. The Christ of Scripture refuses to be an abstraction in the sky. Instead, he chooses to be incarnated in the last, the least, and the lost of this world. I contend that he is especially present in those who suffer from AIDS. Sacramentally, the resurrected Jesus waits to be loved in each of them. Mother Teresa once said, "Whenever I look into the eyes of someone dying of AIDS, I have an eerie awareness that Jesus is staring back at me." Indeed, that is the case. No one can say that he or she loves Jesus without embracing Jesus in those who have this torturous disease.

The indifference on the part of Christians and on the part of the nation in general to those in Africa suffering from AIDS may reveal a latent racism. There is often an unspoken feeling that since these victims of AIDS are usually black people, those of us who are white might just as well look the other way. You can almost sense that there are those who are inwardly saying, *If millions of them die off, will it not relieve the hunger problem in Africa? Will it not eliminate a large proportion of an undesirable race?* I doubt if we will hear those words out loud, but I have heard statements that imply the same thing, and I am horrified! In Christ there is neither Jew nor Greek; bond nor free; Scythian nor barbarian;

"'Lord, when did we see you hungry and give you food, or thirsty and give you something to drink? When did we see you alone and away from home and invite you into our house? When did we see you without clothes and give you something to wear? When did we see you sick or in prison and care for you?'

Then the King will answer, 'I tell you the truth, anything you did for even the least of my people here, you also did for me.'" Matthew 25:37-40 male nor female. Anyone who allows racist tendencies to go unchallenged in his or her personality is not living like a Christian. The Scriptures make it clear that anyone who says he or she loves God and does not love the brother or sister who is a neighbor is a liar. People suffering from AIDS in Africa *are* our brothers and sisters.

Those of us who are in the church must use what moral authority we have to speak against those political and economic structures that the Bible refers to as the "principalities and powers" that rule our age. We must raise our voice against those pharmaceutical corporations that overprice the cocktail drugs that could slow down the effects of the HIV virus in those who are infected. We must call the corporate community to account for their apparent tendency to put profits far above people.

We must also speak out against a government that spends trillions of dollars to build up a military machine but provides only a pittance to deal with the AIDS crisis that is destroying Africa. As we wage war on terrorism, we must be aware that terrorism cannot be eliminated until we deal with the economic imbalances and the social injustices that breed terrorism. When we Americans do so little to help the poor victims of AIDS in Africa, an anger is stirred up that can lead people who are diseased and oppressed to strike at us with vengeance. We do not get rid of malaria by killing mosquitoes. Instead, we must destroy the swamps in which the mosquitoes breed. So it is that we will not get rid of terrorism by killing individual terrorists. In the end, we must get rid of the conditions that breed terrorists. We must attack the poverty and the oppression that nurture such extremism. Enlightened self-interest should lead us to assume that unless we, who live in the richest nation on the face of the earth, respond to the AIDS crisis in Africa, there will be dire consequences.

But, in the end, we who call ourselves followers of Jesus have a higher calling than our own self-interest. If Christ is a reality in our lives, then our hearts will be broken by the things that break the heart of Jesus. There can be no doubt that the heart of our Lord is broken by what is happening in Africa, even now. If nothing else, our hearts should burn within us as we face the fact that thirteen million children in Africa have been orphaned because of AIDS, and that for each of them Jesus sheds his tears.

On Judgment Day, we will not be asked theological questions. Instead, we will be asked, as it says in Matthew 25, how we responded to those who were poor, diseased, downhearted, and alone. Jesus will ask us on that day if we reached out to the stranger in need with loving care and if we treated the sick with true compassion. It is not that theological convictions are unimportant, but rather that true commitment to the beliefs we espouse will be manifested in compassionate action on behalf of those who are writhing in the agonies of AIDS, even now.

Let us remember the chorus of an old gospel hymn:

> *Rescue the perishing,*
> *Care for the dying,*
> *Jesus is merciful,*
> *Jesus will save.*

Written for The aWAKE Project, *copyright © 2002 by Tony Campolo.*

What Can I Do to Help?

Pray for Africa

O God, teach us how to love, how to hope, how to believe in life.

W e pray for healing.

We pray that you will lay your hands on our brothers and sisters of Africa: the mothers, fathers, daughters, and sons. We pray that you will touch their lives with your presence, your love, and your grace. We pray that you will heal their hearts and minds with the gift of life.

We pray that you will heal the Church. We pray that you will touch the hearts, minds, and souls of all religious communities with your compelling hand of truth. We pray that you will heal our fear, our anxiety, and our prejudice that we might live lives of faith, hope, and love to touch those suffering from HIV/AIDS.

We pray for salvation.

We pray that you will lift up our brothers and sisters of Africa from the mire of pain, horror, and disease. We pray that you will offer the gift of salvation to those who are dying. We pray for the living, that you will bless them with hope in the light of love.

We pray for doctors, nurses, caregivers, and researchers. We pray that you will offer them wisdom, compassion, and faith. We pray that you will bless them with an intellect to boldly imagine a world without AIDS, a vision for a new generation of medical care, and an unconditional love for those who are dying without a hope for treatment.

We pray for support.

We pray that you will provide for our brothers and sisters of Africa. We pray that you will comfort them in their time of need. We pray that you will provide food for the hungry, clothes for the naked, a home for the homeless, and medical treatment for those who cannot afford such a luxury. We pray that you will provide your orphans with good families that will raise them in love.

We pray for our governments, our pharmaceutical companies, our corporations, and our religious communities. We pray that each institution will find it in their hearts and minds to offer monetary support by way of funding, medical treatments, and community-oriented aid. We pray that these institutions will advance in bringing "the kingdom come, on earth as it is in heaven" by dropping the debt, providing aid, and promoting trade in Africa.

We pray for compassion.

We pray that you will rain compassion on our brothers and sisters of Africa. We pray that you will instill in the hearts of complacent Americans a vicarious understanding of the suffering—mentally, physically, socially, and emotionally—of those dying with AIDS in Africa. We pray compassion on the cold hearts of those who cling to ignorance and indifference. We pray for compassion on those who are compelled to combat the virus, the suffering, and the death. We pray for compassion for the world as we attempt to wage a war against a deadly disease that is killing our brothers and sisters. We pray for compassion for life itself.

O God, hear our prayer.

Create Awareness among Elected Officials

YOUTH SPECIALTIES, TIM MCLAUGHLIN

B efore you take your case to elected government officials on behalf of Africans with HIV/AIDS, you've got to know *who* they are and *where* to find them. So here's your crash course. Sit yourself down in front of a computer with Internet access, grab your Lucky Charms or graham crackers or licorice whips or whatever you munch while you surf, and let's start.

Your *congressional delegation* consists of your state's two senators and however many representatives it has. The U.S. legislature has two houses: the Senate and the House of Representatives. Every state has exactly two *senators;* a state's number of *representatives,* on the other hand, is determined by that state's population. More populous states have more representatives; less populous states have fewer. (Ask your U.S. history teacher how this came about. Believe us, it's fascinating.)

So if you're from California or New York, say, and want to write all your state's congresspersons, you'll be writing forty-some letters. If you live in Wyoming or Delaware, you'll write three.

Most of these Web sites list your elected officials' snail mail addresses as well as their e-ddresses—and they provide on-the-spot links for e-mailing the official directly from that site.

Here's a helpful hint: Both the Senate and the U.S. House of Representatives have their own Web sites with a wealth of information on current legislation, the annual schedule, and ways to contact your local government officials. Visit them at www.senate.gov and www.house.gov.

FIND YOUR SENATORS
AND REPRESENTATIVES ONLINE

Find your representatives at www.house.gov. From here you can "E-mail Your Representative" or "Contact Your Representative" by clicking the appropriate button.

Find your senators at www.senate.gov. Look for the "Contact Information" button.

Or you can simply go to www.congress.org and find both your representatives and your senators (together, they comprise your state's *congressional delegation*).

Or, of course, if you already know the name of your state's congresspersons, let Google.com find each of their official Web sites (for example, "John Johnson"+senator+home).

Write The Man himself, President Bush, and his VP at www.whitehouse.gov/contact.

FOLLOW LETTER-WRITING PROTOCOL

Don't write, "Dear John . . ." In fact, don't even address the envelope "Sen. John Johnson." How you address some elected officials is as established as driving on the right-hand side of the road (in the United States, at least!). Here are examples; simply replace the names with those of your congressmen or congresswomen:

To your senators:
    The Honorable John J. Johnson
    Start your letter, "Dear Sen. Johnson."

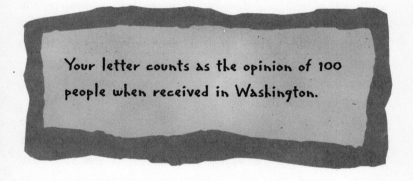

Your letter counts as the opinion of 100 people when received in Washington.

To your representatives:
    The Honorable Audrey J. McElvane
    Start your letter, "Dear Rep. McElvane."

If you're writing the chair of a committee:
    Start the letter "Dear Mr. Chairman" or "Dear Madam Chairwoman."

If you're writing the Speaker of the House:
    Start the letter "Dear Mr. Speaker" or "Dear Madam Speaker."

OK, TIME TO COMPOSE THE LETTER

E-mail or snail mail? Yeah, we know: E-mail is easier than snail-mailed letters. Yet you're dealing with Washington politicians, remember, most of whom wouldn't dream of stepping out their front door for even the morning paper without a suit and tie on. So to a lot of these politicians, handwritten letters are serious letters. But, all it takes is a call to their office to find out if they prefer e-mail or snail mail.

See the sample letter on page 101. (Hey, it's only a sample. Don't go copying it and mailing it, for crying out loud. It is said that some congressional offices equate one handwritten letter with one hundred people who support that issue. If true, that goes to show how influential three or four letters from you can be. It's easy; just follow these tips:

Cut to the chase. After a brief pleasantry, quickly get to the reason for your letter. Be specific, concise, clear, and brief in expressing what action you want your congressperson to take. A couple of paragraphs should do it.

Name the legislation or action. If your letter points to a specific piece of legislation, identify it ("I urge you to vote in favor of H.R. [which stands for "House Resolution"] 95, the Affordable Pharmaceuticals Bill"). To find the name and number of your bill, go online to www.congress.org; under "Issues & Action" click on "Bills in Congress."

Briefly explain why your issue is important. Put the situation in concrete terms ("To withhold inexpensive drugs from impoverished nations is shortsighted, miserly, and contrary to the manufacturers' own long-term interests. Anti-retroviral drugs alone will likely cut the mother-to-child transmission HIV rate in half").

Limit your letter to a single issue. Otherwise you will lose your punch. Stay focused.

September 14, 2003

529 River Drive
Livingston, Montana 59047

The Honorable Audrey McElvane
House of Representatives
943 Longworth House Office Building
Washington, DC 20515

Dear Rep. McElvane:

Congratulations on your reelection a year ago. It's good to have an experienced person like yourself representing Montana.

I am writing to ask you to make affordable HIV/AIDS drugs for Africans a priority. Specifically, I urge you to vote in favor of H.R. 954, the Affordable Pharmaceuticals Bill. Pharmaceutical manufacturers are certainly entitled to make a profit on their products. But in the face of the AIDS pandemic in sub-Saharan Africa—and the one emerging in South Asia—to withhold inexpensive drugs from impoverished nations is short-sighted, miserly, and contrary to the manufacturers' own long-term interests.

Anti-retroviral drugs alone, in a single dose given at birth, will likely cut the mother-to-child transmission rate in half. As it is now, one-quarter of the AIDS deaths in sub-Saharan Africa are of children under the age of five.

Please act now while there is still hope.

Sincerely,

[signature here]
Jason Bridlewell

PHONE YOUR CONGRESSPERSONS TO EXPRESS YOUR VIEWS

Before the call:

- Know your representative's name.

- Know the names of bills currently on the floor in either the House (for a representative) or the Senate (for a senator).

Making the call:

- Dial 202-224-3121 and ask for your representative's office by his or her name.

- When the office picks up, ask for the aide who handles HIV/AIDS relief for Africa.

- Identify yourself with your name and hometown.

- Tell the aide you'd like to leave a brief message. The staffer will remain on the phone and write your message down; they will not transfer you to voice mail. It might be a bit disconcerting at first because they are live on the phone, but just take a deep breath and dive into it. They aren't going to challenge you on what you think.

- Identify your support for, or opposition to, the particular bill in question.

- Give two or three reasons for your opinion.

_____

_____

_____

- Ask for continued support for Africans suffering under the burdens of poor economy, war-torn nations, and the HIV/AIDS pandemic.

- Ask for your representative's stance on the issues at hand.

- Most important, be friendly and respectful (even if one of your congresspersons disagrees with your views), and acknowledge that the aides are handling many different issues.

After you hang up:

- Follow up regularly—call once a month, even once a week. Begin cultivating a relationship with the aide who works on "your" issue.

VISIT YOUR CONGRESSPERSON

Meeting with members of Congress or their congressional staff is a particularly effective way to convey your message about the need for the U.S. government to be a leader in helping address the African HIV/AIDS pandemic.

Of course, if you live in Honolulu or Fairbanks, you probably won't be personally dropping in to your congressperson's office much. Or maybe you still can—members of Congress have home offices in their own districts as well as their Capitol Hill offices. When they fly home to your state for a weekend or a week now and then, they usually make themselves available to their constituents—which includes you! (You can find their home district office addresses and phone numbers in the same places you find their Washington numbers and e-ddresses.)

So call or e-mail your congressperson's office and find out when she'll be where you can see her personally. Then lay the groundwork for your visit:

Plan your visit carefully

Be clear just to yourself about what it is you want to achieve. Determine which member or committee staff you need to meet with to achieve your purpose.

Pre-Visit Prep:

- Call for an appointment. You can call the number in Washington if you plan to meet with your representative there. Or you can look in your local phone book for your representative's hometown offices. When you contact the office, ask for the appointment secretary or scheduler. Explain your purpose and whom you represent. It is easier for congressional staff to arrange a meeting if they know exactly what it is you want to discuss and your relationship to the area or interests represented by the congressperson.

- Research the pertinent bills, media coverage, etc., of the issue you plan to discuss.

OK, you've done the prep work. Now it's the day of your visit:

- Wake up early—you don't want to be snoozing during the meeting.

- Take a shower, use plenty of deodorant and Scope, put on your most businesslike outfit, and look professional. This shows your representatives that you take them seriously; they'll in turn take you seriously.

- Be on time for your appointment—and be patient. Due to congressperson's ridiculously full and overflowing schedule, it is not uncommon for them to be late or for a meeting to be interrupted. So be flexible, be gracious, and, if you must, continue an interrupted or rescheduled meeting with a staffer or aide instead of the congressperson.

- Bring information, materials, and media coverage (newspaper clippings, press releases, videotapes of TV news stories in your hometown) that support your position. Here's why: Congresspersons are required to take positions on many different issues. And because they can't be experts on everything, they lack important details about the pros and cons of some issues. They will be grateful to you for sharing credible information and concrete examples that demonstrate clearly the impact or benefits associated with whatever issue or legislation you're advocating or opposing.

- Be political. Members of Congress want to represent the best interests of their district or state. So wherever possible, demonstrate the connection between what you are requesting and the interests of your congressperson's constituency. Describe how you and your group can assist the congressperson. If it's appropriate, ask your congressperson for a commitment.

- Be responsive. Be prepared to answer questions your congressperson or aide may fire at you, or to at least provide additional or follow-up information in case the congressperson gets interested in your issue and wants more info. Follow up the meeting with a thank-you letter that outlines the different points covered during the meeting, and send along any requested additional information and materials.

Congressional Staff Roles

Members of Congress have staff to assist them during their terms in office. If you're going to be writing, talking to or visiting them, you'd better get acquainted with the staff. Allow us to introduce you to them.

- *Administrative Assistant,* or *Chief of Staff,* reports directly to the congressperson. He or she usually has overall responsibility for evaluating the political outcome of various legislative proposals and constituent requests. The AA is usually the person in charge of overall office operations, including the assignment of work and the supervision of key staff.

- *Legislative Director, Senior Legislative Assistant,* or *Legislative Coordinator* is usually the staffer who monitors the legislative schedule and makes recommendations regarding the pros and cons of particular issues. In some congressional offices there are several legislative assistants, and responsibilities are assigned to staff with particular expertise in specific areas. For example, depending on the responsibilities and interests of the member, an office may include a different legislative assistant for health issues, environmental matters, taxes, etc.

- *Press Secretary* or *Communications Director* builds and maintains open and effective lines of communication between the congressperson, his constituency, and the general public. The press secretary is expected to know the benefits, demands, and special requirements of both print and electronic media, and how to most effectively promote the member's views or position on specific issues.

- *Appointment Secretary, Personal Secretary,* or *Scheduler* is usually responsible for allocating her congressperson's time among the many demands that arise from congressional responsibilities, staff requirements, and constituent requests. The appointment secretary may also be responsible for making necessary travel arrangements, arranging speaking dates, visits to the district, etc.

- *Caseworker* is the staff member usually assigned to help with constituent requests by preparing replies for the congressperson's signature. The caseworker's responsibilities may also include helping to resolve problems brought up by constituents about federal agencies (like Social Security, for example, or Medicare issues, veterans' benefits, passports, etc.). There are often several caseworkers in a congressional office.

Create Awareness in Your Community

GET THE WORD OUT TO YOUR LOCAL PRESS

This isn't difficult—local newspapers are always looking for topical stories with a community angle. So this week it could be your local efforts to stem the African HIV/AIDS crisis. Here are some tips for getting your message disseminated through the media.

WRITE LETTERS TO THE EDITOR

First and most important, check your newspaper's guidelines for submitting a letter to the editor (online as well as somewhere on the Op-Ed pages), and—if you want the editor to look kindly on your letter—conform slavishly to them.

You're more likely to get your letter published in small-circulation newspapers than in major metropolitan papers. Still, if you tie your letter to a recent article, editorial, or column in even a big-city newspaper, you'll greatly increase your chances of getting published.

For example, say your youth group is doing an awareness fund-raising event on behalf of African persons affected by AIDS. Tie your event to a current or very recent event or story in that newspaper—an update on the search for an AIDS cure, perhaps, or a story on the poverty of sub-Saharan countries. Link your activity or news to larger events and news. Better yet: If you can, comment on a specific story in that newspaper, mentioning the headline and date ("In response to your August 14 story 'Charitable Giving Drops in 2002'. . ."). Do an online search on a newspaper's Website to find such articles.

Remember these newspapers, too:

- Neighborhood weeklies

- Your church denomination's regional and national newsletter, newspaper, or magazine

- Local ethnic newspapers, for they are often very interested in issues that affect Latin America, Africa, Asia, and their immigrants in the United States

You can find nearly any newspaper's Web site quickly at newslink.org.

WHAT ANY RESPECTABLE NEWSPAPER EDITOR WILL TELL YOU ABOUT WRITING LETTERS TO THE EDITOR

Conform your letter to the newspaper's published guidelines. Usually this means brief, concise letters of 150 words or so—that's about four short paragraphs. Editors' rule of thumb: The shorter the letter, the greater the likelihood it will be published.

Write with passion. Be controversial. Use strong language, but don't be strident, don't make personal attacks, and stick to swaying readers with the merits of your argument, not primarily with emotion.

Don't shotgun the same letter to several newspapers, unless you are certain that the newspapers serve distinctly different markets. At least give your letters the *appearance* of having been written exclusively for one newspaper.

To Write Powerfully to the Public, Remember EPIC

Instead of spending time figuring out where to begin a letter to the editor, use the EPIC outline—it makes opinion writing much easier and less time-consuming. Use it to organize your ideas and clarify your message.

Engage the reader with a startling fact, a visceral image, or a strong statement of a serious problem.

Propose a specific course of action, a specific piece of legislation, or attention to a specific state of affairs.

Illustrate how the proposal would work and why it's important. Give a few details or examples to make it concrete.

Call your readers to a specific action.

From *www.jubileeusa.org/jubilee.cgi?path=/take_action /get_the_word_out#two. Used with permission.*

Sign your letter, or typically it won't be published. (The exception to this, of course, is e-mailed letters.) An address and phone number are often required, too.

Speaking of e-mailed letters to the editor, they should contain only one e-ddress in the "To" field—that is, don't copy your letter to multiple editors via cc or bcc fields. And send your letter in the body of the e-mail message, not as an attachment.

After you e-mail or snail-mail your letter, be patient. It usually takes at least a week from the time a newspaper receives a letter for it to be published.

The most effective letters are not form letters or copied from form or sample letters—editors can smell such writing a mile away. Write from your heart—a thoughtful letter from a concerned community citizen.

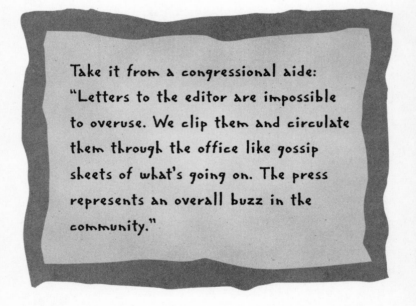

Take it from a congressional aide: "Letters to the editor are impossible to overuse. We clip them and circulate them through the office like gossip sheets of what's going on. The press represents an overall buzz in the community."

Members of Congress subscribe to local newspapers in their districts, which means that you will probably get their attention if, in your letter, you mention their names. To make sure they see your letter, snail-mail or fax a copy to them, along with a brief cover letter. This will reinforce your message.

WRITE A PRESS RELEASE

For starters, take a look at this sample press release. You'll find that its author was a wise and savvy writer of press releases, who religiously followed these guidelines:

PRESS RELEASE   PRESS RELEASE   PRESS RELEASE

For immediate release
Contact: Sylvia Dormicelli, 221-333-9294

Bells Will Ring for Freedom from Debt
Vermonters call on rich country leaders to cancel global debts, save lives
G-8 leaders meeting in Genoa, Italy, has debt relief on the agenda

What: Local activists and religious leaders will be ringing bells at 10 A.M. Saturday, July 21, to call for breaking the chains of debt-slavery that bind more than a billion people.

Where: Gathering at 14th Street and Pearl St. at 10 A.M. with bells and signs calling for debt cancellation for impoverished countries, many of which are ravaged by AIDS.

Vermonters are calling on President Bush and other leaders of the G-8 nations to take another step on the road to full debt cancellation. Several G-8 countries including the U.S. have pledged to cancel 100 percent of the bilateral debts (country-to-country debts) of the poorest countries.

Two years after the initial 100-percent cancellation pledge, only a small portion of the debt has been canceled. The World Bank and the International Monetary Fund (IMF), both of which are wholly controlled by the richest countries, have written off less than half the debts of the most impoverished nations. The World Bank and IMF have sufficient resources to cancel 100 percent of the poorest countries' debts using their own resources and without additional taxpayer funding.

The current AIDS crisis in Africa is taking 5,500 lives every day. The United Nations estimates that $10 billion annually is needed to curb this plague. Meanwhile, sub-Saharan Africa pays out $13.5 million every year in debt service. Savings from debt cancellation can be used for basic healthcare, HIV/AIDS drugs, and clean water.

People traditionally ring bells to mark rites of passage, such as death, marriage, and the end of a war. Local Vermonters will ring bells to draw attention to this important meeting of international leaders and the power they have to proclaim freedom from debt and save millions of lives through deeper debt cancellation.

Bell-ringing events are being held all over the country in timing with the G-8 Summit. The events are organized by the Jubilee USA Network, a broad coalition of religious, labor, and nongovernmental organizations calling for full debt cancellation for the world's impoverished countries. Jubilee USA is the U.S. arm of the global Jubilee debt-cancellation movement, which is active in more than 65 countries.

• • •

Unlike letters to the editor of a newspaper, a single press release can be distributed to as many media contacts as you'd like. Slather the phrase PRESS RELEASE all over the top of the sheet so that any reader—press or otherwise—instantly recognizes what it is.

Give a contact name and phone number at the top of your press release—and be available!

Keep your press release to one page, maximum.

Fortunately or unfortunately, brevity is a high virtue to the media. Get the key facts in the first paragraph: the *who, what, when, where,* and *why* of your event or announcement. For example:

Members of Holy Trinity Church will be ringing their church bells along with eight other Cleveland churches to ring in aid for African sufferers of AIDS. The bell-ringing will take place this Saturday evening at 7 P.M.

Include a local angle, and give names where possible:
Five hundred postcards to President Bush were signed by members of Grace Fellowship of Bingham County, including 12-year-old Jason Brunell and 92-year-old Vivian Green.

Include an occasional, short quote from you or another organizer:
"We want Senator Mulholland to know," said local campaign organizer Kris Johanson, "that most countries that have received debt relief so far are still paying more on debt than they are on health care for their people."

If the press release is about a future event, stress photo opportunities, like this:
Photo opportunity: Dancers from Bingham County's Zambian community will perform at noon on Saturday, March 21, on the County Courthouse Plaza.

If your press release is a recap of a past event, attach one or two photos with full names of the participants.

Make your press release work for you.
Phone the newsdesk of your local newspaper two weeks before the event about the press release to be sent to them, then send the press release a few days later. Phone again a day or two after the press release should have arrived, and encourage the reporter to attend the event—or to at least write a piece on it based on your press release. Don't be discouraged if no one from the press attends your event. Just phone them the day after and

give your own report of events. Arrange to take your own photos of the event, and send the best ones (with a copy of the press release) to your local newspaper.

Politicians monitor local press, for it gives an indication of public opinion on current issues. But just to make sure they get the message, send a copy of any articles that are published in the press, with a letter, to the relevant decision makers.

Engage Your Community's Adults

Start with your own parents. Talk with them about what you've learned. Give them copies of press releases you or a friend have written about the African AIDS crisis, and ask if they will post them at their workplace—in the lunchroom, on the office bulletin board, etc.

Post these same releases on the bulletin boards of community colleges or universities in your town.

> Not everyone will be as passionate about the AIDS crisis as you are. Prepare to be met with skepticism and apathy. But don't let others discourage your drive in assisting with this worthy cause.

When it's appropriate, talk up the African AIDS crisis—and what you or your group is doing about it—in whatever Internet chat rooms you frequent. When you instant-message friends, ask them what they know about the crisis—and be ready to give 'em some stats. (Use the ones you see throughout this book.)

Ask your pastor if your youth group can organize a Sunday morning church service—or at least part of one—to familiarize your congregation with the AIDS pandemic in Africa and how they can help. See the sample "African AIDS Awareness Sunday" (pages 116–129) for what such a church service could look like.

Sign up to speak at your town's city council meeting as a citizen, and urge the council to adopt a resolution to do their part in alleviating the AIDS pandemic in Africa. Generously season your brief statement with up-to-date stats from www.unaids.org.

MOBILIZE OTHER CHURCHES IN YOUR HOMETOWN

Take your "African AIDS Awareness Sunday" service (see following) to other churches in your community. Call the pastors—better yet, make personal visits to them—in order to thoroughly explain the need and how your service can help. Having your pastor make the first contact may be helpful. It may also be a good idea to make an audio or even a video recording of the service when you first present it at your church so you can hand the cassette or CD to interested pastors of other churches.

Many communities, cities, and counties have networks or associations of youth workers and pastors who meet monthly. Ask your youth worker or pastor if you can attend one of these network meetings with them, and use that opportunity to promote your own church's "African AIDS Awareness Sunday" or to arouse interest in having that service in their own churches.

HOST AN "AFRICAN AIDS AWARENESS SUNDAY"

Hosting a church service is one of the most powerful ways you can impact your community regarding the HIV/AIDS crisis in Africa. Here's what you need to do:

- Call your youth pastor and tell him you want to do this as a youth group.
- Go with your youth pastor to your senior pastor and set up the date. You'll probably need to have the materials below prepared for this meeting.
- Find ten to fifteen youth to help with the worship service.
- Contact some local musicians who specialize in African music (or have a group of students use bongo drums, etc.) to help with the worship that Sunday.
- Contact your missions staff at church or other missions organizations to see if they have any video footage from trips to Africa.

Here is what the church service could look like:

- Sing two songs with great rhythms to get the congregation warmed up.
- Open with the prayer for Africa on page 95–96 of *Mission: Africa*.
- Have some readers read stats from *Mission: Africa* from the podium.
- Sing more songs then read a story from the "Real Stories of Real Zambians" section (starting on page 122). Follow this pattern until you have read all the stories.

- If you were able to get video footage, show these clips throughout the service.
- Close with a prayer for Africa and take a collection to be donated to a charity.

Be sure to engage a full range of emotions in the congregation. Describe the horror of the current AIDS crisis, but also tell of the beauty of the African country and the courage of the African people. Don't concentrate solely on the problem, but also offer solutions and ways that the congregation can become involved.

Conduct the following Bible study among yourselves—"Great Pairs That Never Should Have Split Up: Sonny and Cher, L.A. and the Rams, Preaching and Healing" (Matthew 9–10; Luke 9)—then use appropriate parts of it to make a case before the congregation of how healing is still an essential part of the gospel.

Great Pairs That Never Should Have Split Up: Sonny and Cher, L.A. and the Rams, Preaching and Healing

A Bible study in Matthew 9–10 and Luke 9
The aim of this Bible study is to broaden your assumptions about what healing is. For specifics, see "Talking Points" at the end. Use relevant points or pieces of this Bible study in your church service for driving home the point that healing is still an essential part of the gospel.

Read these Bible verses:
> Matthew 9:35
> Matthew 10:1
> Matthew 10:5, 7–8
> Luke 9:1–2

1. How would you respond to someone who said: "Like, duh, isn't it obvious that preaching and healing were two halves of Jesus' ministry—and not just his, but of his disciples' ministry, too?"

_____
_____
_____
_____

2. In what ways (if any) can you say that modern disciples of Jesus are still in the healing business?

_____
_____
_____
_____

3. What kind of lines do you draw when it comes to God's healing people? Can you always recognize God's hand in healing? Does God even have a hand in healing these days? Rate your feelings with a mark on the line below.

← ── →

| When God heals, it is always supernatural—today as well as in Bible times. | Sometimes God heals, sometimes the doctor heals. It's always one or the other. | It's difficult to separate God's part in healing from human efforts. There's a lot of overlapping. | Sure, in ancient times God certainly healed people miraculously. But no more. To heal us these days, he gave us antibiotics and high-tech surgical procedures. |

Notice how the two are mentioned together in the same breath: "preaching the good news and healing disease and sickness." Did you catch the specific mention in Matthew 10 about healing those with skin diseases? It's often in skin tumors that AIDS shows itself.

TALK ABOUT THIS . . .

Why do we assume that we modern-day disciples of Jesus can drop the healing half of the preaching-healing equation? That all we have to do is preach or share the gospel?

_____

_____

_____

_____

What if one mark of a disciple is to heal, by whatever means you are capable of? With Jesus that way was miraculous. Now, perhaps, there are other ways. Do nonmiraculous ways of healing mean they are less important? Or can the healing be *emotional* healing?

_____

_____

_____

_____

_____

Jesus plainly told his disciples (among other things) to heal the sick. Just because we can't do *all* the things Jesus commanded of them—like raise the dead—does that let us off the hook of doing what we *can* do?

FINALLY . . .

Is there anything in any of the verses on page 118 that's a puzzle to you or that just doesn't make sense?

_____

_____

_____

_____

_____

What one thing got your attention most of all in these verses? Why did it affect you as it did?

_____

_____

_____

_____

TALKING POINTS FOR
FOLLOWING UP ON THIS BIBLE STUDY

1. Preaching and healing just kinda always went together, at least from what we read in the Gospels.

2. Jesus demonstrated this one-two punch (preaching *and* healing), and he wanted his disciples to use it, too.

3. There's no biblical reason to limit healing to only miraculous healing. Granted, when Jesus healed he used his hands, his power, and a prayer, not a syringe and a dose of antibiotics. And what healings we read about that his apostles did were similarly supernatural.

But read between the lines for a moment.

Take a look at Acts 16:6–12. (Go ahead . . . we'll wait while you look it up and read it. Finished? Good.) What's with the shift from *they* to *we?* One minute Luke is writing, "Paul traveled here and did that, and they finally arrived at Troas," and a sentence later it's all, "The next morning we left Troas by ship and arrived at Philippi, and we stayed there."

Most theologians agree with the obvious solution to this pesky pronoun problem: that Luke joined Paul's missionary entourage when it arrived at Troas.

Furthermore, we know from Colossians 4:14 that it was likely this same Luke (the writer of the Gospel book as well as of Acts— think of those two history books as First Luke and Second Luke) who was also a physician by training. And we know that Luke was with Paul during at least some of his prison terms (see Colossians 4:10, 14, 18; 2 Timothy 1:16; 4:11; Philemon 1, 13, 23–24).

So Paul may have performed his share of miraculous healings, but the biblical record points to his needing a good old-fashioned doctor to stay by his side. If you remember, the apostle was constantly getting beaten up, stoned, whipped—and those are just the occasions we know of. It is a very good guess that Paul didn't supernaturally heal his own wounds at such times but trusted the diagnoses, salves, herbs, and compresses of his dear friend and MD, Luke.

All that fascinating Pauline detail to say this: Healing is healing, with whatever resources are at hand. This was true in first-century Judea and Macedonia, and it is just as true today in Spokane and Chattanooga. It may be ibuprofen in your medicine cabinet, dollars in your wallet donated for an AIDS cure, a massage with your hands, or the healing power of God in your voice. Whatever you have, heal with it.

REAL STORIES OF REAL ZAMBIANS

Childhood Lost: Teenage Boy Cares for Sisters Orphaned by AIDS
Scariot Banda

He gave up his childhood just so he could give his sisters hope and a better future. Since his parents' death from HIV/AIDS-related illnesses, Richard Kaunda has not deserted his two sisters Winnie and Catherine, like their six older siblings did ten years ago. Richard, who resides in Zamtan, does jobs for people to raise money to meet his needs and those of his two sisters.

When his parents died, Richard was only eight, Winnie was six, and Catherine, the youngest, was four. Today, ten years later, Richard has become their father and mother all rolled up in one.

After the death of his parents in 1991, three of his siblings, whom they had been staying with, left for different places. Three others, who were living elsewhere at the time of their parents' deaths, did not bother to take care of these youngest three or take them into their homes.

After being abandoned, they spent some time at their grand-father's home. "During the day, we would spend time at his place, while at night we would go back to our house," he said. But unfortunately the grandfather died a few years later. They have been living in his home since.

Richard dropped out of school because there was nobody to help pay for his school fees. There were times when the family had to go without food because there was nothing in the house and there was no money to buy groceries.

In order to sustain the family, Richard worked different jobs for families. He helped some in their maize fields, for others he helped to make bricks, dug pit latrines and rubbish pits, and drew water. After completing the tasks, they would either pay him with goods or cash.

Today, while his friends are in school trying to get an education, Richard is still out earning an income so that his family does not perish from hunger. He has been working at his neighbor's poultry farm. When his friends are heading for school, he heads for Mr. Sichela's poultry place. "Mr. Sichela is one of the few people in Zamtan who has everything going for him, and I want to be like him one day," Richard remarks. "He does not need to worry about how he is going to take care of his family."

But Richard realizes that success comes only through hard work and getting an education. He regrets not continuing with his secondary education but intends to see that his sisters complete school. Winnie is now in grade nine and will be taking her junior secondary exams in November, while Catherine is in primary school, grade six.

Because he knows his parents died from HIV/AIDS, he is remaining abstinent until he gets married. "I was told that the safest is to totally keep away until I get married," he remarks. He also is protective of his sisters. He wants them to finish school and not to get mixed up with boys as they also can get AIDS.

World Vision's project has helped advise the community on the need for their children to complete their education and the dangers of HIV/AIDS. Richard is also aware of this campaign, and the advice he has for his sisters is that when asked for sex or any kind of relationship with a boy, "Refuse, run, and tell me!"

When a Child Becomes "Mom" to a Child
Alfred Chirwa

Mutinta Hasibesu, eight, has dropped out of school to look after her seven-month-old brother, Nchimunya. The two orphans are currently living with their mother's sister Mrs. Lingamba, who took them in after their mother died of a prolonged illness last May. When Mutinta was brought in to live with her aunt, she was in her first grade at a nearby primary school.

But life changed for Mutinta. She had to quit school in order to baby-sit her brother, because her aunt had her own infant to care for. Mutinta now does household chores fit for an adult and does not have time to play with children her own age. She is too busy looking after Nchimunya.

> So many children in Africa are forced to take on adult responsibilities. Take a moment and pray for them now.

On a visit to World Vision's Twachiyanda area development program in Zambia's southern province, it was discovered that Mutinta had walked eighty kilometers (nearly fifty miles) carrying her brother on her back to the nearest hospital. She had accompanied her aunt, whose child was ill. On the trek, Mutinta and her brother were exposed to the harsh environment, as well as infections and disease. After her aunt's child had been discharged from hospital, Mutinta had to walk back eighty kilometers (almost fifty miles) to their village with her brother on her back.

A Princess with a Vision for AIDS Sufferers
Charles Kachikoti

Princess Kasune Zulu, twenty-six, says point-blank that her parents died of AIDS. She is not sure when she caught it, but she learned of her HIV–positive status while married in 1997.

This would be one of those usual stories about the ravages of the world's most invincible disease pandemic. But it's not, because this victim has a vision. Princess has a vision to redeem from silent paralysis and helpless fear all HIV / AIDS sufferers and carriers and has already started pursuing it in a big way.

She has become World Vision Zambia's special envoy on HIV / AIDS, if she can be called that, and has a countrywide mandate to speak to all classes of people on the pandemic. She has, since 2000, run a series of radio talk shows and has been featured at major functions of corporate executives. She has not merely made speeches but has set up a home for orphans and a number of organizations tackling the plight of the poor and AIDS victims.

Born on January 6, 1976, to Joyce Mwanamusulwe and Godson Moffat Kasune, Princess came face-to-face with AIDS when her mother died in Liteta Hospital, Chibombo, in the central province of Zambia in October 1993.

Recently, her oldest brother died in Chibombo, leaving behind two children, one of whom she is caring for. Princess is responsible for looking after her grandparents and three orphaned cousins, as well as her younger brothers and sisters. One of her brothers just completed high school, but she is unable to send him on to college, which has effectively derailed his ambitions to become a journalist.

Princess Kasune Zulu has devoted much of her means and influence to help the cause of HIV/AIDS sufferers. With your own current financial status, consider what you would be willing to devote to this cause. Choose a worthy charity or organization and make a monthly financial pledge.

"People kept saying my mother died of witchcraft and depression," Princess observes, "but I know it was because of AIDS. I think even Mum knew she had AIDS, because she wrote a will." Princess believes that had her mother told her about AIDS, she may not have caught it.

Asked about how she was infected with HIV, Princess says directly and firmly: "Naturally there was a lot of peer pressure [to have sexual intercourse] when I was a schoolgirl. The death of my mum and dad contributed to even greater pressure. I don't know how I got infected. I was not a virgin when I got married," she says.

Her doctor told Princess that she needs anti-retrovirals because the number of CD4 cells in her body has slumped drastically. The difficulty, she says, is that for the purpose of using anti-retrovirals she needs 330,000 Zambian kwachas (about $82) to cover a CD4 count test, CD8, and viral load at UTH. Similar tests thereafter again call for more payments, excluding the actual price of the medicines.

Princess has two children, Joy, who is seven, and Faith, who is six, and five stepchildren. "We have tested our children for HIV three times. They are negative. Dr. Manasseh Phiri has said, 'This is a miracle from God,' and I agree. I have educated my children about HIV as young as they are."

CAMPAIGNS

In 1997, Princess and her husband, Moffat, gave up their Luanshya house to set up a community school—the Fountain of Life School. The house in New Town has been the site of educational work spearheaded by the voluntary work of Sharon Lombe and her husband, a local pastor. Princess is happy that her five stepchildren have personally helped to draw water for the children in times when taps have run dry. A well presently exists in the yard as a response to prolonged droughts in the region.

Princess would like to sell the home-based school building and buy a new and bigger house to serve more children. She says in times past some children fended for themselves by working in the yards of miners' residences and assisting charcoal burners. Miners and charcoal burners provided the much-needed income. Today, her vision is to see that the school-age children don't suffer from illiteracy.

She adds emphatically: "We should educate people on the sin of fornication and the power of virginity. The Bible principles have much to say on awareness, prevention, and care for the ill as well as hope for the dying. For me to live is the grace of God. I shall not die but live and proclaim the grace of God."

Princess says when she discovered her HIV status in 1997, she embarked on a plan to honor her Savior, Jesus Christ, by disclosing her status and talking about it to society. In the beginning, Moffat was against it. Only much later did he comprehend the gravity of matters and also came out into the open about his own status. He also speaks at a range of gatherings.

"The Stanchart Ndola branch were the first to allow me to speak to their employees; I spoke there twice and once to the Kitwe branch, where I spoke to the management. I have also spoken to the Zambia National Building Society in Luanshya," Princess explains.

Her husband, Moffat, has lost two jobs in circumstances she feels were related to management's rejection of him because of his HIV-positive status. Since then it has been tough going, but they have seen the Lord provide for them.

Moffat says, "Life has changed in the sense that hope is emerging for people living with AIDS. Three support groups for People Living with HIV/AIDS (PLWA) have been revived, where they meet and share their experiences. She also provides tips on positive living while using herself as an example."

Now that Princess advocates abstinence as her main message, she is asked if people are really able to abstain, and she says, "It is possible; it is not possible." She explains: "What I mean by this is that as much as the church is preaching abstinence, people are still not abstaining. The first thing is that people should abstain by appreciating the power of virginity and putting God first above their feelings. Abstinence should be promoted. But if people are already living together and they are not married, or if they are married, they should be faithful to each other."

Princess advocates an anti-AIDS campaign where the church preaches according to what it knows best, and educators also crusade according to what they know best. Youths and adults alike should be told that the condom, while available, is not 100 percent safe. Conflicts over methods of preventing the spread of AIDS are, she feels, needless.

Given the gravity of the AIDS pandemic, Princess prefers that the schools' curriculums include HIV education. It is in this way that the spread of AIDS can be slowed down drastically.

And before AIDS slows Princess and Moffat, they are on the warpath. Their war cry shall be heard because their vision is becoming more visible to more people. It is a vision that one princess has passionately committed her life to.

Raise Money

You've spread the word throughout your community about the bad times in Africa. You've written your elected officials asking them to take strong political positions in favor of African AIDS relief issues. Now shut down your computer, turn off your phone and go put on some work clothes—because it's time for raising some money yourself for the sake of Africans affected by AIDS.

FIRST THINGS

But don't ask for a cent until you *plan*.

1. Write and agree on a purpose statement.

Not only will this give you direction as you plan the fundraiser, but it's a clear, brief, explanatory way for you to introduce your cause to a prospective donor.

It could go something like this:

The Borscht Community Church youth group is raising $1,500 for African AIDS relief. The money we collect will pay for a year's worth of food for four widows and their children who are forced to provide for themselves after their husbands died of AIDS.

A number of free resources on the Web will offer further help in writing your purpose statement. Do a quick search using "purpose statement" or "writing a purpose statement" and you'll find several links. In addition, reading the purpose statements of existing organizations or charities can be extremely helpful.

Note that the purpose statement tells prospective donors about your organization, why you're doing what you're doing, and how much cash you're gunning for.

2. Choose the right fund-raiser.

Decide how you will raise the money. Will you plan a group fund-raiser, like a car wash or a booth at a community winter carnival? Or do you want to each go your own way and solicit donations from friends and relatives? What past fund-raising efforts have worked for your group? What has bombed? What kind of fund-raising works best in your church or community— a good ol' candy sale, a Saturday night spaghetti feed in the church basement, a neighborhood window-washing you do for a fee, or a performance you charge admission to?

Let these questions help steer you to a fund-raiser that raises funds to the ceiling for you:

- How much money can you realistically raise by this means in your community?

- How much work will it take to raise the needed money?

- Is this idea consistent with the policies and ideology of your organization?

- Are there more effective ways to get the money you need?

- Do you even have the resources to pull off this fund-raiser?

- How's the timing? What's an appropriate date for the kind of fund-raiser you want to do? How much lead time will you need to prepare for it?

- How excited is your group about this fund-raising idea?

For a few ideas to get your fund-raising juices flowing, see "Some Fund-raising Ideas" later in this section.

3. Be a team.

Some in your group are better at making cold contacts door-to-door. Others are exacting record keepers. Still others are better planners than executors. So divide your group so all are working in their areas of strength.

Remember, the particular service or item you are offering in a fund-raiser is not as important as the cause you are promoting. Whatever fund-raiser you choose, be sure that you are making customers aware of the AIDS crisis in Africa.

Then fill in this chart:

Name of Fund-raiser _____

Date _____

Fund-raising Task	Person(s) Responsible	Date to Be Completed	Estimated Cost
1. _____	_____	_____	_____
2. _____	_____	_____	_____
3. _____	_____	_____	_____
4. _____	_____	_____	_____
5. _____	_____	_____	_____
6. _____	_____	_____	_____
7. _____	_____	_____	_____
8. _____	_____	_____	_____

4. Select a chairperson.

This isn't the one who does the most work, but the one who keeps all the workers efficient. You may want to consider an adult in your congregation or community who has fund-raising experience. A college student with a couple of years of organizational leadership on her campus may be all you need—or perhaps a retired businessperson.

5. Promote your fund-raiser.

Think posters . . . fliers . . . press releases to local media . . . announcements in church meetings and services . . . even public-service announcements on radio and TV, as well as inviting reporters to write straight news stories on your event or campaign.

> In addition to posters, fliers, press releases, etc., be sure to get plenty of grass-roots, word-of-mouth promotion. Seeing a poster may spark someone's interest, but a personal invitation may be what is needed to get them to attend.

6. Stay legal.

Make sure you obtain any permits or permissions that may be necessary. Read any contracts thoroughly, especially clauses regarding liability insurance. If you don't run a contract by an attorney friend, at least make a phone call to someone with legal expertise who can walk you through terminology and help you understand what the contract says.

7. *Calculate your costs in advance and keep accurate records.*

It costs money to raise money. The trick is to spend less than you raise. Prior planning and ongoing documentation will help you pull off this trick.

8. *Time your event wisely.*

Check the church, school, and community calendars in order to avoid conflicts. You want prospective donors in town, undistracted, and not having just given to a fund-raiser held a week ahead of yours.

9. *Follow up.*

Say thank you appropriately: at least at the moment of the donation, then with a note or postcard if possible, or in printed announcements in your church program, bulletin, or newsletter. Every once in a while over the next couple of months, publish or announce updates on the progress or the results of your fund-raising efforts.

SOME FUND-RAISING IDEAS

If garage sales, car washes, and bake sales do the trick, go with 'em. But also try to find creative ways to raise the money: Dare your students to eat PBJs instead of McDonald's for a month, to give up soda, or to cancel their cable TV for a month.

If you've had success selling merchandise, be sure to check out www.fundraising-ideas.com/fundraisers/index.html for everything from cookie dough to coupon books to sell. If you want to go to friends, neighbors, and relatives to simply and directly solicit money for one of the One Life Revolution catalog items, the Web page www.oneliferevolution.org/help/catalog/howto.html walks you and your youth group through the easy process of collecting money and sending it to World Vision. Or check out any of the gazillion fund-raising ideas in books and articles specifically for youth groups.

Here are a few fund-raisers that may be a little different from what you're used to.

> If your fund-raiser involves selling something (a bake sale, a food booth at a local fair, etc.), see if local businesses would be willing to donate some or all of the supplies you will need. With a mention at your booth in exchange, they may be willing to join a worthy cause. It never hurts to ask!

AFRICA AWARENESS TARIFF

Raise your congregation's awareness about how many material things they possess—and raise money at the same time. Write, design, and distribute a calendar for a given month: Scatter facts about Africa, AIDS, etc., among the weekday squares (pull those facts from the earlier section "Create Awareness in Your Community"). And in the Sunday squares, print the tariff your youth group will levy on that day so parishioners can come prepared to pay up.

For example, charge a tariff based on the number of TVs in a home, number of shoes in the household, number of vehicles (count cars, RVs, boats, snowmobiles, motorcycles)—whatever makes your congregation aware of how much they have compared to typical sub-Saharan Africans. For shoes, say, charge a household one dollar for each pair of shoes above one pair per householder.

THE SPIRIT OF AFRICA COOKBOOK

Compile a simple cookbook of recipes that reflect at least ingredients native to Africa. These can include foods and recipes from Latin America, the Caribbean, and the American South (slavers' destinations, where black slaves adapted aspects of their cooking to New World circumstances). Once you're assured of lots of authentic recipes, take preorders—then print 10 to 20 percent more cookbooks than your total preorders.

AIDS AWARENESS THEATER

There are many scripts, short and long, suitable for readers' theater or straight drama. Plan ahead, spend a couple of months in rehearsal, make a set as minimal or exotic as you want. Promote it shamelessly and communitywide with brochures, fliers, and mini-performances of a scene at Rotary, PTA, and church meetings. Also do interviews with local media—including lots of information from you about the use of the admission price. Perform it Friday through Sunday nights for two weeks. Serve a dessert and coffee for a special touch.

For scripts, ask any high-school drama teacher if you can borrow their script catalogs, which list scripts by topic (among other ways).

The All-You-Can't-Eat Fund-raising Dinner

Sponsor a moneymaking dinner by—well, by not having one. Yeah, you heard right. This is especially appropriate to famine-plagued Africa.

Here's how it works. Ask people to contribute a predetermined cost for the dinner, but tell them they don't have to bother attending—which frees you from the organizing hassle of cooking food. All you have to do is sell tickets.

Invest a little of what you save from not having to buy and prepare food on donor thank-yous. Create an award on cardstock that looks framable and give it to all who buy tickets to the non-dinner—maybe something like this:*

HONORABLE MENTION

BILL THOMPSON
didn't make a pig of himself
at the
2nd Annual Leafton Church
All-You-Can't-Eat Dinner

Adapted from the supremely helpful Great Fundraising Ideas for Youth Groups by David Lynn. Used by permission.

Send Stuff

S o what do you do now with all that moola you raised to help remedy the African AIDS crisis?

First of all, lose the idea of sending care packages of Band-Aids, cans of stewed tomatoes, and slips of paper printed with Bible verses (although Band-Aids, tomatoes, and the Bible all have an important place in people's lives). Your first task is to choose an organization through which to funnel the money to Africa—an organization that will spend the money in ways that give Africans the most valuable assistance.

Take World Vision, for example (www.worldvision.org). Compelled by the AIDS crisis in sub-Saharan Africa, this international child-aid organization decided to focus on one country—Zambia—in which to invest and concentrate its efforts. So World Vision conducted on-site research and conversations in Zambia, plus consulted all the latest research, including very thorough work by UNAIDS, the Joint United Nations Programme on HIV/AIDS (www.unaids.org).

The conclusion that World Vision arrived at: The last thing Zambia needed was a fix from outside their own country and culture. Even if World Vision raised a billion dollars and bought

AIDS drugs with all of it, there would remain huge logistical, domestic, and cultural obstacles.

> It is extremely important that you do your research. Make sure the organization you contribute to is reputable and effective. Believe it or not, not every organization that claims to be "charitable" is. There are seedy groups out there who are willing to make a buck off the suffering of others.

So World Vision decided against Big Brother flying into Zambia with crates of drugs and hundreds of doctors and whatnot. Besides, they kept bumping up against this reality: Children develop best when they are able to remain with their siblings within a family situation with an adult caregiver in their own community.

USING THE FAMILIAR

It was found (to no one's surprise) that the comfort of siblings, relatives, familiar authority figures, and surroundings helped ease the grief, insecurity, and fears experienced by children who had lost a parent. When orphans can stay in their own community and with their own siblings, they are able to fully participate in their own

How One Organization Is Spending Money in Africa

World Vision's Five Strategic Objectives

This is how World Vision decided to use donated money in Zambia. Notice how most of the details supporting these objectives deal *within the framework of existing Zambian social structures* instead of dumping a lot of anti-AIDS drugs on villages with no way of storing or administering the drugs, or sending planeloads of U.S. doctors to administer those drugs, only to have those same doctors fly out of the country a month later and leave the Zambians alone again to cope with all the ripple effects and ramifications of AIDS.

Strategic Objective 1

Increased food security for households of orphans and vulnerable children (OVC) by:

- Helping farmers improve crop production,

- Helping households get access to a wider variety of nutritious foods,

- Helping households increase their income (by raising poultry, goats, sheep, hogs, cattle, and selling eggs, milk, offspring, etc.),

- Helping Zambians retain assets after a parent's death (by advising communities of legal rights and wills, by reporting property-grabbing to police, etc.).

Strategic Objective 2

Reduced HIV infection among fifteen- to nineteen-year-olds by:

- Creating AIDS-awareness and AIDS-education groups and clubs and classes,

- Using these groups to promote abstinence, faithfulness, and good reproductive health,

- Starting these clubs and classes in public and church schools,

- Helping protect six- to seventeen-year-old females from sexual abuse and early marriage,

- Encouraging twelve- to seventeen-year-olds to use youth-friendly health services (including STD/HIV counseling, testing, and treatment).

Strategic Objective 3
Psychosocial support for OVC by:

- Establishing youth recreation programs,

- Recruiting and training community and church volunteers to visit OVC households and do psychosocial counseling or grief counseling.

Strategic Objective 4
Age-appropriate education for OVC by:

- Persuading schools to waive fees and uniform requirements for OVC,

- Persuading Zambian community groups and churches to cover school costs for OVC,

- Building schools and training teachers for those schools,

- Linking OVC who are out of school with local tradesmen for apprenticeships,

- Establishing community day-care centers for one- to six-year-old OVC, and training volunteer day-care staff in nutrition and development,

- Reducing OVC workloads and scheduling work outside of school time (by drilling wells closer to villages, by constructing more fuel-efficient stoves so OVC don't have to gather as much wood for cooking and heating, by church and community volunteers helping OVC with firewood collection and child-care duties they may have).

Strategic Objective 5
Delayed orphaning through home-based care for persons living with AIDS by:

- Arranging for community and church volunteers to make weekly visits to persons living with AIDS,

- Training these volunteer caregivers in nutrition, hygiene, safety, and the basics of HIV/AIDS.

traditions and cultures. Which means, in turn, they are more likely to succeed in school and get prepared for their future livelihood.

Hence, World Vision's idea: Plow whatever money they can collect into a community mobilization strategy to strengthen community-based institutions and families. In other words, the organization would empower society to take responsibility for the well-being of orphans and vulnerable children affected by HIV/AIDS. The strategies would strengthen *existing* resources, coping mechanisms, and support capabilities within the extended family and community structures. (Why reinvent the wheel if you can use what is already working?)

So World Vision gave itself these marching orders:

- Help increase awareness among students and youth groups about the problems facing Zambian orphans and vulnerable children;

- Then assist students and youth groups around the world to strengthen or create Zambian structures and processes that will support the households of that country's orphans and vulnerable children.

World Vision is calling this effort "One Life Revolution," and to make sure that whatever bucks you raise for Africans gets used in ways that make a big difference, they have an online catalog.

So go shopping! Here's a summary of materials, services, even livestock that you can put your hard-earned dollars toward (www.oneliferevolution.org/help/catalog). All of these purchases are designed to give the African recipients long-term resources and hope that will last. These are practical, useful items for widows and orphans who have been affected by AIDS—and their communities.

HEALTH CARE

Care for a Child—$50

Includes food, transportation to school, hope, educational support, nourishing food, and one-on-one adult assistance and counseling

Health Care Provisions for a Child—$25

Provides mosquito nets, emergency care, medicine, health care, and comforting protection

Clean Water from a Well—$8,000

Offers improved health to a community of 360 people and access to safe water and sanitation, which affects a community's ability to break the vicious cycle of poverty and reduces the child-mortality rate by half

DAILY NEEDS

Blanket—$15

Warmth for a child

Home Construction—$3,000

Construction of a two-room home for a family with vulnerable children

Food for a Mother and Orphans for One Year—$380

Daily meals to children and mothers who are forced to provide for themselves after a father dies of AIDS

FINANCIAL SECURITY

Two Goats—$30
Dairy goats for a household of orphaned children—milk, cheese, and yogurt for consumption and income

Vegetable-Growing Kit—$100
Gardening tools, fertilizer, and six types of vegetable seeds for consumption and income

Vocational Training for a Child—$1,200
For children raising children, vocational training in order to support younger siblings and cousins—pays for one child who has lost one or both parents to learn construction, tailoring, automobile repair, or other trades

Small-Scale Poultry Raising—$55
For consumption and income, ten chickens and wire fencing to start small poultry-production operation

HOPE FOR A FUTURE

Three-Room Schoolhouse—$53,000
Makeshift shelters and outdoor classrooms replaced with a new school building—benefits will continue to flow when an entire community is educated

One Year of Education for a Child—$120
For OVC unable to afford the cost of attending school, one year of tuition for one child

Youth Club for One Year—$1,500

A place for Zambian youth to learn facts about AIDS and AIDS prevention, lifesaving behaviors, reproductive health education, and general life skills and to be involved in community service, recreation, and sports

Sponsor an Individual African Child

There are many child-aid agencies, and the two with the widest influence just may be Compassion International and World Vision.

Through Compassion International (www.compassion.com), for $28 a month, you (or your family or youth group) can sponsor an African child. Here's what your monthly support for "your" child does through Compassion:

- Gives the child a variety of educational opportunities,
- Offers the child the chance to develop numerous life skills,
- Supplies medical support and supplemental nutrition as needed, and
- Develops the child's self-confidence and social skills.

Compassion's goal is to break the cycle of poverty by providing assistance to children around the world on four levels—spiritual, physical, economic, and social. Plus, Compassion supports children only in towns where it has a close relationship with native pastors, teachers, and missionaries. They team with local churches to implement their programs, working within the cultures of numerous people groups worldwide.

World Vision (www.worldvision.org) does a very similar thing for children, for $26 per month. Both agencies allow you to choose the child or children you want to support based on country, gender, etc.

DIRECT CASH

If you want to make a one-time cash donation instead of providing ongoing support for a child or two, both Compassion International and World Vision can channel your cash into whatever kind of project you choose.

For instance, you can give to Compassion's "Help for Child Victims of HIV" fund (click on the "Make a Contribution" button), which provides AIDS awareness programs to help native staff, partners, and families understand and prevent the disease. And for those who have already contracted the disease, the fund offers critical resources, including medicine and dietary supplements.

Make the most of your donation!
Compare different organizations and
what they're able to provide with a
specific amount of money. Look for
special options like World Vision's
gift-match program.

World Vision has a special donation category for vulnerable African children: Whatever cash gift you give will be doubled (thanks to a private grant), so that your $40, say, will double to $80—and that's enough to give two African children a school uniform (necessary in many African schools), a backpack full of school supplies, and a year's tuition. (Sweet deal, especially if your youth group could raise $160—which would double to $320—thereby giving *eight* children these educational things that will help give them life options and help them out of poverty.)

World Vision also has related causes for which you can earmark one-time contributions: Ethiopian drought victims, the South African food crisis, and AIDS orphans throughout the world.

UNAIDS (that would be the Joint United Nations Programme on HIV/AIDS, at unaids.org) has an "Apathy Is Lethal" campaign (www.apathy-is-lethal.org) to which you or your youth group can make a contribution. It will help provide care for those currently infected, support for educational programs to stop the spread of infection, and support for those families who are affected by disease.

It's all good stuff. And there are lots of others, too. Check with your church for what your denomination may be doing that you can contribute to. Check with your city's African-American organizations, which are usually aware of AIDS relief measures aimed at Africa as well as at your own city.

How to Get a Passport

Start by checking out the U.S. State Department's Web pages about passports—everything you need to know is here: http://travel.state.gov/passport_services.html. The following info is a very basic, general, and partial summary of this site. So be the first teenager on your block to get a passport of your very own! Here's how:

1. Download an Application for Passport form (DS-11) at http://travel.state.gov/download_applications.html, and complete it (except for the signature, which you must do in the presence of an official). Or you can just obtain the form at the passport office and complete it there.

2. Find the nearest place you can apply for a passport—usually city and county government buildings (county clerks, city treasurer, records departments, etc.) and main post offices. (Use the U.S. State Department's locator at http://iafdb.travel.state.gov.)

3. Take with you:

- Your completed passport application, unsigned,
- Your birth certificate,

- ID (usually a driver's license),
- Two passport photos of yourself,
- $85 (a little less if you're under 16)—a check is best, and
- A parent with ID (if you're 17 or younger).

For details, qualifications, and shortcuts, see
http://travel.state.gov/passport_services.html.

CHOOSING YOUR DESTINATION IN AFRICA

There's a veritable abundance of things that can go wrong during
a visit to Africa. At the time of publication, the U.S. State
Department had warnings of varying degrees of seriousness
against traveling pretty much anywhere in East Africa, especially
in Kenya, Zimbabwe, Tanzania, Somalia, and Berundi (read 'em
at http://travel.state.gov/warnings_list.html). Online travel site
LonelyPlanet.com posts warnings for pretty much all of East
Africa, too: Somalia, Kenya, Rwanda, Berundi, Mozambique, and
Zimbabwe.

Still, there *are* East African countries that the State Department
and travel companies claim are relatively safe: Uganda and Zambia,
for example (as long as you don't venture near the borders). But
even in these nations the political situation could change overnight.
So do your homework. Better yet, let an experienced and savvy
tour group do much of the homework for you—which bring us to
the next point:

CHOOSE YOUR TREKKING
COMPANIONS WISELY

Don't even think about going to Africa by yourself. Go with an
organization that is experienced in African travel, offers a variety

of services to facilitate your trip, and has reliable African connections to create a worthwhile trip and keep you safe.

Maybe your youth group wants to go all together . . . maybe you are the only person in your youth group who wants to go to Africa. In either case, hook up with an organization that's savvy in all things African. Here are some places to start:

> Be smart. You will be more helpful to the people in a region where you and your supplies are able to get in safely. You are not a secret agent—know your limitations. Leave the guerrilla warfare tactics to those who have more experience in areas that are least safe.

- *Compassion International* (www.compassion.com) is a worldwide children's agency that aims at "releasing them from their spiritual, economic, social, and physical poverty and enabling them to become responsible and fulfilled Christian adults." Its Overseas Tours Program gives sponsors the opportunity to see their sponsored children face to face in Africa, Asia, and Latin America.

- *Action International* (www.actionintl.org) is an "evangelical, nondenominational missionary-sending agency that works in major urban centers of Asia, Latin America, and

Africa." When you visit their Web site, click on "Short-Term Mission Opportunities," which often include two-week stints in East Africa.

- *Wycliffe* (www.wycliffe.org) is a family of missionary organizations, having grown up around the original Wycliffe Bible Translators. On their Website, click on the link for "Get Outta Town" or "Short-Term Mission Opportunities." Plus, for eight bucks you can get their *Guidebook to the Road Less Traveled,* a how-to workbook about short-term missions as well as a discipleship tool to prep you for the experience ahead of you.

- *CWM Youth* (www.cwmyouth.org) is an arm of the Council for World Mission. If you're out of high school and a twenty-something, you may be eligible for their "Training in Mission," a one-year training program in South Africa and India.

- *Mission Finder* (www.missionfinder.org) is a "classified directory of Christian mission opportunities." Click on "Short Term" for a meaty list of organizations, missions, and groups that offer short-term mission experiences. (A recent search pulled up thirty-five short-term opportunities in Africa.)

"Jesus said to his followers, 'Go everywhere in the world, and tell the Good News to everyone.'" Mark 16:15

Finally, a word to the wise: Keep your parents and your youth pastor in the loop. Even if you're the only student from your youth group who has the initial interest in visiting Africa, you just may ignite an adult's imagination enough to start a groupwide trip.

THOSE PESKY VACCINES

The Centers for Disease Control recommend the following vaccines for travelers to East Africa (see www.cdc.gov/travel/eafrica.htm for details). See your doctor at least four to six weeks before your trip to allow time for shots to take effect.

- *Hepatitis A* or immune globulin (IG).
- *Hepatitis B*, if you might be exposed to blood (for example, health-care workers), stay longer than six months, or be exposed through medical treatment.
- *Rabies*, if you might be exposed to wild or domestic animals through your work or recreation.
- *Typhoid*, particularly if you are visiting developing countries in this region.
- *Yellow fever*, if you travel anywhere outside urban areas.
- As needed, booster doses for *tetanus-diphtheria, measles,* and a one-time dose of *polio* vaccine for adults.

WHAT HEALTH AND BEAUTY SUPPLIES SHOULD YOU TAKE TO EAST AFRICA?

First, leave the eyeliner and Clearasil at home. Think safety, not sleekness. Second, the travel pros at LonelyPlanet.com say not to leave home without a small medical kit that includes:

- Aspirin for pain or fever
- Antihistamine (such as Benadryl)—it's useful as a decongestant for colds and allergies, to ease the itch from insect bites or stings, and to help prevent motion sickness. There are several antihistamines on the market, all with different pros and cons (for example, a tendency to cause drowsiness), so it's worth discussing your requirements with a pharmacist or doctor
- Antibiotics are useful if you're traveling well off the beaten track, but they must be prescribed—and you should carry the prescription with you
- Loperamide (Imodium) or Lomotil for diarrhea
- Prochlorperazine (Stemetil) or metaclopramide (Maxalon) for nausea and vomiting
- Rehydration mixture for treatment of severe diarrhea—especially important if traveling with children
- Antiseptic such as povidone-iodine (Betadine) for cuts and scratches
- Multivitamins, especially for long trips when dietary vitamin intake may be inadequate
- Calamine lotion or aluminium sulphate spray (Stingose spray) to ease irritation from bites and stings
- Bandages and Band-Aids for minor injuries
- Scissors
- Tweezers
- Thermometer
- Insect repellent
- Sunscreen
- ChapStick

- Water purification tablets
- Cold and flu tablets
- Throat lozenges
- [a] Pseudoephedrine hydrochloride (Sudafed) may be useful if flying with a cold to avoid ear damage
- A couple of syringes and needles, in case you need injections in a country with medical hygiene problems; ask your doctor for a note explaining why they have been prescribed

(From www.lonelyplanet.com/health/predeparture.htm#imm. Used with permission.)

By taking a trip to Africa you would be embarking on a journey you'll never forget. But if God's calling you to help from home, that's a noble effort, too. Spend some time with him and see what he leads you to do.

DONATIONS

All contributors have generously donated their royalties to the following organizations, and Transit has matched their donation.

AWAKE

www.AWAKEproject.org

AWAKE connects the church with facts and resources about the African AIDS emergency. Our vision is to awaken the Christian community to greater action on issues of justice and mercy worldwide.

WORLD VISION'S HOPE INITIATIVE

www.worldvision.org

The Hope Initiative is World Vision's global response to reduce the world-wide impact of HIV/AIDS. Introduced in October 2000 and officially launched in March 2001, the Hope Initiative will expand and enhance World Vision's HIV/AIDS programming in all of the countries where it works.

The aWAKE Project

UNITING AGAINST THE AFRICAN AIDS CRISIS

Nelson Mandela
Bono
George W. Bush
Jeff Sachs
Women of Faith
Mark Schoofs
Bill Frist
Kevin Max
Helen Epstein
Tony Campolo
Dikembe Mutombo
Kofi Annan
Danny Glover
Philip Yancey
Nadine Gordimer

The aWAKE Project is a collection of stories and essays geared toward educating readers to the crisis in Africa caused by the AIDS virus. aWAKE stands for: AIDS-Working toward Awareness, Knowledge and Engagement. Compiled of articles written by significant speakers on the AIDS issue, ranging from Nelson Mandela to Kevin Max, *The aWAKE Project* provides poignant stories and compelling statistics, encouraging the reader to care and even take action to battle this horrific crisis.

W Publishing Group™
www.wpublishinggroup.com

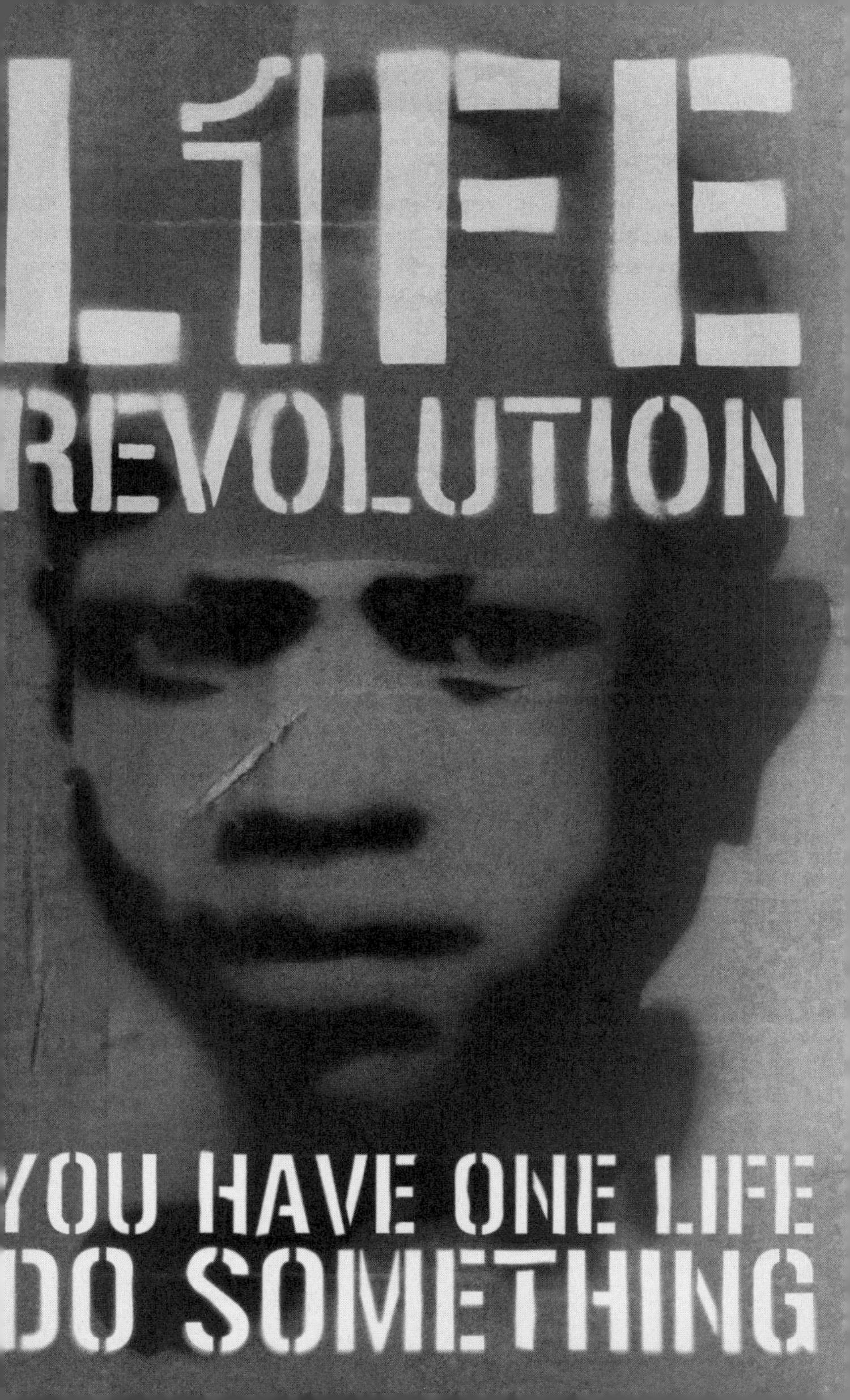
1LIFE
REVOLUTION
YOU HAVE ONE LIFE
DO SOMETHING

ONE LIFE
REVOLUTION

The Revolution has begun.

Consider this your call to action. Hundreds of thousands of students like us are beginning a fight that can quite literally save an entire generation from extinction—and change the course of history.

We're talking about going up against a killer...of the likes the world has never seen: AIDS. Mothers and fathers are dying every day, leaving millions of children orphaned and alone.

We're taking a stand. Now.

ONE LIFE: YOURS
TO SAVE ONE LIFE: AN ORPHAN, A WIDOW
FROM ONE DISEASE: AIDS
IN ONE COUNTRY: ZAMBIA

Why Now?

We're tired of the fear. We're tired of adults who retreat from the issue. We are tired of being told we can't do much, and we are tired of being told to be cautious, to be careful, to be safe, to wait.

This generation is tired of waiting. We want to act now. We are ready to get our hands dirty, empty our pockets, and sacrifice our time and our energy to touch the innocent victims—vulnerable children and widows—with help and hope.

This isn't your parents' fundraising event. It's not some generic, vague, make-me-feel-good money raising project. And it's not about helping some do-good company stay in business. This is a practical, people-centered effort that is controlled by YOU. YOU decide how to spend the money by selecting catalog items you believe will help care for those children and widows left behind. Inside is a catalog of hope, full of practical, make-a-difference opportunities to change the face of AIDS. Now!

Stop the suffering brought on by AIDS. Join the Revolution.

World Vision

Youth Specialties

Food for a Mother and Orphans for One Year

Provide daily meals to a hungry family! Children and mothers who are forced to provide for themselves after a father dies of AIDS, struggle to have enough to eat. With your purchase, a mother with two or more children will have the comfort and security of knowing that they will have the means to survive.

8662 **$380**

Blanket

Even in Zambia, nights can be cold. Wrap a child in a soft, cozy blanket for warmth and security. Your purchase will comfort a child, and a good night's sleep will help her to be stronger and healthier. 8669 **$15**

ealth Care Provisions r a Child

lespread HIV/AIDS makes vast numbers eople vulnerable to other killers like aria. Mosquito nets, emergency care, dicine – these simple items can save s! You can give a child health care, nforting protection – and life itself – ugh your purchase.

8661 **$25**

www.oneliferevolution.org

Vegetable Growing Kit

Gardening tools, fertilizer, and six types of vegetable seeds will help a vulnerable family meet its nutritional needs and sell extra produce for income. The right tools are key to preparing and working the Zambian land for planting. Provide these basic elements for a life-giving successful harvest.

8665   **$100**

Small-Scale Poultry Raising

Fresh eggs! A great source of nutrition and a reliable income source for children who have so few options in life, living in villages that have been ravaged by HIV/AIDS. Provide 10 feathered friends and wire fencing to start a small poultry production operation.

8660   **$55**

Clean Water From a Well

Clean water does more than quench thirst. Access to safe water and sanitation affects a community's ability to break the vicious cycle of poverty. It also reduces the child-mortality rate by half. Your purchase offers improved health to a community of 360 people.

8666   **$8,000**

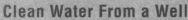